GROWING
GREAT BOYS

GROWING
GREAT BOYS

Ian Grant

Vermilion

7 9 10 8 6

First published in 2006 by Random House New Zealand

First published in the UK in 2008 by Vermilion, an imprint of Ebury Publishing

Ebury Publishing is a Random House Group company

The Random House Group Limited Reg. No. 954009

Addresses for companies within the Random House Group can be found at www.randomhouse.co.uk

A CIP catalogue record for this book is available from the British Library

The Random House Group Limited supports The Forest Stewardship Council (FSC®), the leading international forest certification organisation. Our books carrying the FSC label are printed on FSC® certified paper. FSC is the only forest certification scheme endorsed by the leading environmental organisations, including Greenpeace. Our paper procurement policy can be found at www.randomhouse.co.uk/environment

MIX
Paper from
responsible sources
FSC
www.fsc.org   FSC® C016897

Printed and bound by CPI Group (UK) Ltd, Croydon, CR0 4YY

ISBN 9780091923525

Copies are available at special rates for bulk orders. Contact the sales development team on 020 7840 8487 or visit www.booksforpromotions.co.uk for more information.

To buy books by your favourite authors and register for offers visit www.randomhouse.co.uk

Contents

Dedication

I dedicate this book to three boys who have grown up to be great men — Andrew Grant, Jonathan Grant and Craig Heilmann — whom I am now honoured to call my friends, and to five grandsons who have taught me so much, and who I know will grow into great men — Joshua, Samuel, Jonty, Noah and Christoph.

I would like to thank all the men who, over the years, have taken the time to mentor me and for the lessons they have passed on. I would also like to thank John Cowan, my colleague and friend, whose writings spill over in various ways into this book.

Finally, a huge thank you to my precious Mary who contributed so much to this book, through being a superb mother to our sons. A man could not wish for a better companion and gracious advisor. You are one awesome lady.

Foreword

Ian Grant has a genuine gift for getting to the heart of what concerns and challenges all parents as they experience the joys, the excitement, the wonder and the worries of parenting in the new millennium. He has a warm and deep understanding of the human condition.

Growing Great Boys is a delightful 'manual' for successfully guiding, coaching, coaxing, disciplining, loving, encouraging and inspiring boys from birth through to their teenage years. Its substance is insightful and challenging and it will be rewarding to all parents who read it.

While firmly emphasising the importance of both mother and father in the parenting roles, and pointing out the different and essential contributions both make to a young boy's life, Ian provides special advice on and encouragement for the father's role. 'Fathers are not male mothers, they have a parenting style all of their own,' Ian says. And, 'Every boy needs a male in his life to download the software of how to be a man.' And, 'You've got what it takes, son!'

The book's format presents logical themes running through each chapter that culminate in twelve cornerstone pieces of advice that parents can leave with their sons and know that they will be successful, positive, contented men. The advice given is based on Ian's lifelong involvement with young people and family life, his wide reading of distinguished scholars on parenting, and on his bringing up his own daughter and two sons. The book provides guidance, advice, opinions, humour, anecdotes and practical solutions in an inspiring and cheerful manner. It is neither patronising nor judgemental but, rather, heart-warming and encouraging.

Growing Great Boys is a book 'for all seasons' — every parent, every family, whatever age, stage or condition, whoever they are, will find this book fascinating reading. It is a scholarly book which does not trivialise the issues that parents face but shows a deep and warm understanding of the special relationships between parents and growing boys. This relationship and the development of strong, united, caring families is surely one of the most important challenges, if not the most important challenge, facing all nations in the years ahead.

Ian Grant's book provides genuine answers to this crucial challenge and adds another chapter to his lifelong contribution to the wellbeing of young people and families in New Zealand and throughout the world.

It is a privilege to have been invited to write a foreword to this important book.

D. J. Graham C.B.E.
Former Headmaster, Auckland Grammar School
Former Chancellor, Auckland University
President, New Zealand Rugby Football Union
Chairman, Parents Inc. NZ

Introduction

Growing boys is better than fixing men

I am convinced that this generation of boys, like those before them, have every reason to grow into young men who give manhood a good name. However, there are some special challenges for boys growing up today, unique to our technological and individualised 21st-century society.

I am well aware of the many books already in the marketplace addressing the issues of boys' successes and failures, and documenting helpful research. However, this little book is of a different genre.

I spend my working days, through seminars, toolbox parenting groups, radio spots and magazines, giving parents insights and ideas for the daily interactions that take place in their homes. I deal in offering parents 'hot tips' that are practical, and that work in real life. It is this user-friendly information that I offer in this book, in the hope that some of the ideas will mean it becomes a valuable 'how to' in raising your sons.

Without doubt, our world needs men who have a healthy and authentic view of their masculinity, strong, courageous and protective, yet also able to live an emotional life that nurtures the inner person. Empathy and altruism are personal qualities that, from the earliest times of societal development, have been considered the building blocks of conscience and character. These attributes are a worthy goal for our sons.

Like any other generation of boys, our sons' futures lie to a significant degree in the hands of their parents. As mentors and nurturers, we have the great privilege of being the 'big people' who set boundaries, create a positive atmosphere and show loving commitment.

Each of our sons is a gift; their personality and DNA are unique to them. When we draw back and study our small sons, as an astronomer studies the stars, we can acknowledge the person each was born to be, then coach him towards his strengths.

Not all boys will be the testosterone-fuelled, physical, sports-mad macho types, but there is a strong likelihood that your son will be somewhere on a spectrum of 'physicalness' that challenges most mothers and needs to test itself against a dad.

For many years, during which we have seen more than 150,000 parents attend our programmes at Parents Inc. in New Zealand, I have been encouraged by how many have grabbed the concept of becoming a parent-coach, identifying with this role of training their children to succeed in the game of life.

My hope is that you, as a parent, will realise that *you* are the builder of your boy's life. Everyone else is more like a subcontractor on your parenting journey.

What an investment! As you see your boy grow into those qualities that Michael Gurian, in his book *The Good Son*, calls 'the true measures of a man' — compassion, self-discipline, decency, honour and empathy — you will know that you have contributed not just to one boy's life, but to the whole community, and to the future.

I wish you well on your journey.

Ian Grant

Chapter 1

The landscape for boys in the 21st century

A boy is wisdom with bubble gum in his hair ... the hope of the future with a frog in his pocket.

— Anon

I have just returned from a wonderful few weeks visiting my adult children and five special little grandsons, on two continents. To be perfectly honest, I'm a little exhausted, but feeling really good. I have played rough-and-tumble games, fixed toys, replaced a zillion batteries, walked (or, rather, run) beside miniature learning cyclists, kicked balls, pulled kids on blankets around polished floors and told all my favourite bedtime stories several times over (and over) by special request.

In reconnecting with these little boys, I have experimented with some grandparent to grandson 'male bonding'. Armed as I was with perhaps more perspective, time and knowledge about the nature of boys than I had been as a dad, I was conscious about communicating some of the definitive 'boy messages' vital to every little boy's sense of identity.

I ensured that, woven into all the games we played, was the key message every male wants to hear — 'You've got what it takes, son.'

Whether it was a 'high five' as a game began, the granddad's 'thumbs up' code of approval (especially when one of them began to lose it), or the little chat on the sideline that let them know I understood, I consciously built this underlying message into all my interactions. It was amazing how quickly a boy who was affirmed in this way recovered his composure.

I am convinced that, if we wish to recover for boys of this generation a sense of identity and mission, we must parent them with certain things in mind. We cannot turn the clock back and nostalgically re-establish the ways of the past. We must capitalise on what can be positively embraced by sons in their culture, and protect them from the violent and salacious. We must lend them our eyes and our perspective, and give them boundaries until they themselves learn to be discerning and morally strong.

There is something special and magical about boys. Every parent of a boy notices, for instance, that their personalities and wiring are different from girls. Left in the back garden to play, they will think up action games, climb trees or create mock battles. They love action and heroism. They love to be challenged physically and to be part of a team. Boys are the ultimate explorers and adventurers, and often display exuberant energy — creating challenges for parents in our urbanised society.

Although many aspects of our modern world are different from the past, some things never change. One is that boys will always need to be parented in different ways from girls. Of course I'm not referring to the basics, such as what we expect from their character and behaviour. What I mean is that, because of their unique hormonal drives and wiring, there will be challenges that boys face that are different from those faced by girls. These biologically programmed differences have now been thoroughly researched, and reassure us that what parents of boys have observed and concluded over the years, about boys' physicalness and less verbal tendencies, are very real and based in physiology.

Michael Gurian, author of *The Wonder of Boys* and *The Good Son*, explains how the male amygdala, the primary aggression centre of the brain, is larger than that of the female and creates more active aggression in males. He suggests that 'when this fact is applied to male hormonal and cultural life, we find a deep and basic clue as to why boys get involved, so much more than girls, in morally "at risk" behaviour — more aggressive or violent behaviour. For instance, a boy is more likely than a girl to hit, more likely to curse or otherwise compete with or one-up another person as a way of relating. It's important to remember, however, that aggression and violence are not the same thing.'

The natural impulsiveness that boys tend to display is also rooted in their biology. The lower levels of serotonin, the chemical that pacifies and calms, in a boy's brain mean he has less impulse control than a girl has. This means that a boy must be given clear moral boundaries and firm discipline, and helped to live with this natural tendency by understanding that his actions have consequences. It may mean that we have to be very patient, and display persistence and consistence as he gains the self-control and maturity he needs.

However, I would like to say, right at the outset, that those impulsive and exuberant tendencies that you as parents often find so challenging in toddler boys are likely, in the end, to be the very things you are most proud of in your adult sons. The men who winch themselves down steep cliffs to rescue stranded accident victims, and the good men who provide for the next generation through doctoring, building roads, teaching or coaching sport will, to some extent, be the result of your nurturing and coaching. But their biology will be the fabric with which you work.

> Those impulsive and exuberant tendencies that you find so challenging in toddler boys are likely to be the very things you are most proud of in your adult sons.

These 'boy tendencies' towards impulsivity, passion and protectiveness have taken a hammering in the past few decades from a feminist climate that has left many men, along with their sons, floundering for an identity and a role in the post-feminist, sexualised culture.

Doris Lessing, the famous novelist and feminist, recently made an observation on how this radical view was damaging to young boys. 'I was in a class of 9- and 10-year-olds, boys and girls, and this young woman was telling these kids that the reason for wars was the innately violent nature of men. You could see the little girls, fat with complacency and conceit, while the little boys sat there crumpled, apologising for their existence, thinking this was going to be the pattern of their lives.' We must give our boys an identity they can be proud of, and a valued role in the world.

Parenting boys will challenge our resourcefulness. They will teach us things that we may never have known, and they will explore the world in their own boyish way. However, when a boy is understood and given emotional support, you will see the best qualities of manhood emerge — and be honoured to call this loyal, passionate, stoic, hard-working, sensitive, fearless and strong human being your son.

A recent incident illustrated for me how the physical expression of play is both vital and enjoyable to boys. I had taken my two grandsons to a playground at Palm Beach on Waiheke Island in New Zealand. When we arrived, four boys were playing barbadoor (bull-rush or, if you're English, 'bull dog'). It's a competitive, rough-and-tumble game, involving running through a space trying to avoid being tackled by those in the centre.

As we watched the children play I chatted with a woman who I assumed was the mother of all the boys. When I asked her about her sons, she replied, 'Oh no, I'm only the mother of one.' She then continued to tell me how her family, on holiday from Sweden, had come to the park a few days previously with their young son, who soon made friends and got involved in this game with the local boys. She said, 'It has made such a difference to my son. We have now cancelled part of our touring to stay here a few days longer, because he's a totally different boy. You see, in Sweden, boys don't play rough, competitive games like this.'

We may think that, by protecting our boys from rough and tumble, we will avoid future violence. However, many experts believe that the reverse is true: boys who are not allowed to enjoy the harmless rough-and-tumble games of boyhood actually become violent in other ways.

By capitalising on what we know about the dreams of boys, we can understand those things that motivate them. As John Eldredge explains in his best-selling book *Wild at Heart*, we can respond appropriately to boys' deepest desires. In the heart of every little boy is the longing to be someone to be reckoned with; to be valiant and strong. He longs for a battle to win, an adventure to live and a heroine to rescue.

That's why my little grandsons, along with all little boys, dress up as Batman, Superman, Buzz Lightyear or The Incredibles — because they know 'there are baddies in the town', and someone needs to 'get' them. The protector and defender in a small boy wants to be assured that he is 'up to it'. These children will not grow into violent adults. It is far more likely that, if mentored with compassion and wisdom, they will grow to become surgeons who work long hours to save lives, or firefighters who rush into burning buildings to rescue people.

Yes, boys will be susceptible to becoming brutalised if we tolerate media violence in our homes, or fail to monitor bullying or gratuitously violent video games, but we must not confuse this type of violence with the little boys in the back garden with the homemade sword and all the paraphernalia that goes with mock battles. Since long before the days of Robin Hood, the 'goodies' winning over the 'baddies' allowed boys to act out their childhood fantasies of protecting their home territory from the bad and the evil.

HOT TIP ✔

THREE VITAL GIFTS PARENTS CAN OFFER BOYS TO HELP THEM THRIVE IN TODAY'S HIGH-PRESSURE WORLD

Security
A boy will feel secure when he knows he is a valued part of the family team.
- Give him tasks, celebrate his milestones and his steps towards achievements, so that he is valued for his contributions.

Self-worth
Self-esteem comes from a sense of progress.
- When your son knows that he is capable of making good choices

by himself, as opposed to just carrying out instructions, self-worth will come from the inside.

- Offer messages that lock-in love such as 'I like it when you think for yourself', or 'It's OK to make mistakes — that's how we learn.'

Significance

Give your son the gift of individuality and choice.

- Ask for and value his opinions. Listen and debrief, in an adult way. When he has had a hard time, offer him your 'adult' perspective.

However, what is new for this generation, as my family is currently experiencing, are the increasingly global world, where families sometimes live on different continents, and the technology-driven, ever-increasing pace of modern life. So much has changed since our own childhoods, it feels as if someone has pressed the 'fast-forward' button and, for that reason, we have to be street-smart with parenting our boys.

Because of the fast pace of change that the world has experienced over the last decades, many experts acknowledge that there are sometimes real challenges to finding a wavelength with our children, who may be better versed in how to programme a computer than how to pitch a tent. Robert D. Strom, Ph.D, an Arizona State University Professor of Psychology in Education, Family Resources and Human Development, has found that there is an ever-widening 'generation gap' between the young and, especially, the elderly.

'When older people of today were children,' Strom explains, 'the world was changing less rapidly. Consequently, in those days, a father might reasonably say to his son, "Let me tell you about life and what to expect. Now, when I was your age . . ." Because of the slow rate of change, children could see their future as they observed the day-to-day activities of parents and grandparents.'

But something happens when the use of technology in a society begins to accelerate. The rate of social change also increases. Therefore, according to Strom, 'Successive generations of grandparents, parents and children have less in common.'

Children today are having experiences that were not even part of their parents' upbringing. And so, says Strom, 'the traditional comment to children — "You're too young to understand" — has been reversed. Today, there are some things adults are "too old" to know, and recalling one's own childhood as the basis for offering advice has become less credible.'

However, amid all this change and pressure, I want to encourage parents that their job is still highly significant, and irreplaceable. We have in our hands the credible tools to launch loving, responsible young men into the world — men who are contributors, not just takers; men who will defend the weak, build teams, provide well for their loved ones and display moral leadership. It seems so much more sensible to build boys rather than to fix men. We really only get one shot at it — so let's make it our best.

In fact, if you don't put the effort into your child's development when he is small, then you will have to later on. When taking the time to discipline and follow-through with a young son, I often joked with my wife that this effort was going to save lots of time on future prison visits!

Seriously though, research suggests that, by the age of seven, future violence and criminality in boys can often be predicted. So if a boy is showing signs of bullying, cruelty to other children or animals or extreme anger it is very wise for parents to give him special attention. This means providing quality time, re-establishing strong bonds with a male figure if possible, and letting him know that he is a worthwhile human being. Setting strong boundaries, giving him strategies to handle his emotions, along with consequences that are logical and reasonable to deal with misdemeanours, will all be important to get him back on track.

We must not settle for less, and we must expect good things of our boys. Let your son know that he is a better person than his current behaviour indicates, while coaching him towards the adult you dream he will become.

I recently read a book about sons of wealthy parents who, in the midst of privilege, had grown into wonderful caring, contributing adults. All the parents interviewed, without exception, said that from day one (many even before their children were born) they had decided to take the time and effort to concentrate on their boys' character; to teach them empathy, thoughtfulness, care for others and an ethic of giving generously to others in gratefulness for their own circumstances.

They took them to work in soup kitchens, taught them to volunteer and to mentor younger boys. It would be fair to say that Princess Diana modelled some of these activities in a powerful way with her two boys as they were growing.

These parents had struck on a vital truth. Our families need to stand for something. When our boys are born, they should be joining a family that already has its own mission or direction in life. Modern western families too often see children as an end in themselves, and re-orientate everything around this little person. However, for a child, real security is joining a family that already knows what it stands for and has a purpose and vision.

Every boy needs a sense of mission and belonging, and your own family's altruism and generosity will build into that innate sense. Encourage your son by saying, 'I am so proud of you, son, the way you noticed that Max was being left out (or 'the way you let our visitor choose the best bike', or 'the way that you were patient with the little kids while they were learning the game'). That shows real character!'

I was fascinated recently to be a silent witness to an interaction between a small boy and his mother. This adorable child had always been naturally cooperative and, since he was verbal at a very young age, avoided to some extent the common frustration and tantrums of the two-year-old. However, now, as a three-year-old, he has developed a huge personality, with oscillating emotions and big opinions.

After being sent to sit on the 'thinking stair' because of a misdemeanour, I heard him crying and muttering, then calling out at the top of his voice, 'I'm going to grow up to be a baddie.' In his little mind, there was no doubt that the worst way he could hurt his parents was to grow up to be a 'baddie'. You see, everything he had learned and knew was that goodness, kindness and protectiveness were to be affirmed, and badness was to be vanquished.

Sadly, I have to say that I have spoken to many wealthy fathers struggling with their sons' rejection — in some cases, rank hatred — of them, fathers who thought they were giving their sons everything by providing the toys (big and little), the holidays, the private education and the economic security. But they were never there for their son when he needed a parent-coach to say, 'I'm so proud to have you as my son, but we don't talk like that in this house.'

Your son has to hear from you, his parent, in a thousand different ways, the words 'You've got what it takes, son.' Every problem he faces, every difficulty you help him to own, can be supported by this message: 'You can solve this, because you've got what it takes.'

When he comes home discouraged from a sports event because he didn't play well and the team lost, you could say, 'Get over it, it's only a game,' or you could build resilience and a can-do message by empathising with the result, while affirming progress. 'Well, your skills are certainly improving. Everyone has bad days sometimes. With more practice, you will become more confident. Remember, it's OK to do something badly while you are learning. You'll become a real champion before you know it, because you've got what it takes, son.'

Adversity and lack of success can actually be a catalyst for growth and celebration. In his book *Raising Children at Promise*, Dr Timothy Stuart tells how he turned a high school, in a very low-decile area, around from failure and 'at risk' to one that now has one of the highest graduation and success rates in the USA. By viewing each student's potential as if through a magic-eye picture, and ignoring the obvious or first appearances, he was able to believe that in the soul of each child was a dream that God had planted in their hearts.

Stuart lists seven characteristics that he believes build 'promise' in a child:

- Perseverance.
- Responsibility for our actions.
- Optimism.
- Motivation through identity.
- Integrity.
- Service.
- Engaged play.

Stuart specialised in teaching his students to refuse to allow labels that come from their assets or deficits to form their identity. Adversity, he believes, provides a catalyst for a child's character growth, and that character is dependent on a good mentor. In adversity, a trusting relationship with a caring adult will help a child interpret that adversity and use it as a stepping stone to build strong character.

IN SUMMARY 👁

HOW TO VALIDATE 21ST-CENTURY BOYS

Boys need:

- A sense of belonging. They need parents who have a strong sense of what their family stands for and who are secure enough to take charge.
- A sense of purpose — they need to be involved in family meetings, rules, mottoes and mission statements.
- Affirmation of their deepest dreams.
- High expectations and a high level of support from their parents.
- Lots of opportunities for fun, adventure and physical challenge.

Chapter 2

Real differences
– real boys

The crisis of masculinity is part of a much larger cultural
crisis, a crisis in our attitude to the modern world itself.

– *Tom Morton,* Altered Mates

Our boys are nothing if not morally fragile, from the inside
out. And there are ways in which our boys are simply more
vulnerable than girls to moral instability. To neglect this fact
is to neglect our boys.

– *Michael Gurian,* The Good Son

What is a male worth? One of the positive outcomes of research
conducted over recent years is that the misunderstanding
and misreading of boys has been put in context. The unique
physiology and psychology of boys is not something to be emasculated or
to rescue them from, but to be channelled into healthy manhood.

What does it mean to have a son?

The greatest tragedy is to view boys as simply noise machines — uncaring, uncommunicative and uninvolved — whereas deep within the soul of every little boy is the hero; a little Huck Finn or Tarzan wanting to pit his strength physically against the odds, and longing for approval and appreciation of his uniqueness.

Many experiments have highlighted the different ways used by little girls and boys to relate to others. Even before they are born, baby boys are more active physically. After eight weeks' gestation, testosterone begins to kick in and starts to bring about physiological changes in boys. Newborn girls will concentrate on faces and language, while baby boys will be attracted to moving objects. Language development is slower in boys, and many parents will observe that they use sounds, such as motor noises, far more than actual words. In their developing speech, nearly all of the sounds little girls make tend to be verbally communicative, whereas with boys only something like 40 percent are verbal; the rest is just noises.

When small boys and girls are playing with blocks, the boys will build structures that are bigger and higher, using more space, whereas the girls will build houses and set up tea parties. Boys will head for the trucks and sandpit at kindergarten, whereas girls will gravitate towards the dress-up box or the playhouse.

Boys are stronger, with 30 percent more muscle bulk on average than girls. They have more red blood cells, and need more physical activity. Their brains grow more slowly, with fewer connections between the right and left hemispheres. (This is why boys' speech faculties develop more slowly than do those of girls, and why men recover more slowly from strokes!)

Researchers in the USA undertook a fascinating experiment. Assuming that there was no great biological difference between boys and girls, they expected to prove that conditioning was the major influence on young boys' behaviour. They left boys and girls together in a room, with only Barbie dolls to play with. They had assumed the children would play similarly with the dolls. But their observations proved surprising. While girls cuddled, dressed and manicured the dolls, the boys were only interested in finding out how well the Barbies would work as torpedoes, bombs or airplanes!

This activity is actually related to how boys' brains function. Boys tend to explore their environment by running, jumping, touching and opening, because their brain is structured in a way that is more orientated to the external world than the internal. Even the way boys show happiness and distress, often through physical 'acting out', is different, and the instruction to 'use words not fists' can be less simple than it sounds for a little boy to process.

A young boy's brain matures more slowly than a girl's, so he may not be ready for school as soon. Studies also show that a poor start may leave him struggling for years, so if his parents feel he is not socially or intellectually ready, holding a boy back may sometimes be appropriate.

After many years of political correctness, as a society we are at last acknowledging what parents have known all along — that boys and girls are different. The consensus among scientists and sociologists is that boys are 'wired' in different ways from girls. In fact, every single cell of their body is programmed differently, from the womb.

> It seems that, as a culture, we are not clear who and what men and women are, or how they should be acting.

But it seems that, as a culture, we are not clear who and what men and women are, or how they should be acting. It's as if we have become embarrassed for boys to be boys. This confusion is then passed on to our sons.

The best research shows that healthy social development of both boys and girls requires the input of two different-sex parents. This is because there is a fundamental difference between the sexes, and both mothers and fathers contribute to a child's identity in different ways. The blurring of gender lines only confuses young people, who are developing their own identity. Read the following chapters on a father's role, a mother's role and single parenting for more on these different roles and how they can draw strength from each other.

Dr David Popenoe, Associate Dean of Social and Behavioural Sciences at Rutgers University (USA) writes in his book *Life Without Father*, 'The burden of social science evidence supports the idea that gender-differentiated parenting is important for human development, and that the contribution of fathers to child-rearing is unique and irreplaceable. A broad review of psychological research in the journal *Child Development*, for example, concluded that children of parents who are sex typed [with clear gender distinctions between mother and father] are "more competent" . . .

'The significance of gender-differentiated parenting undoubtedly is related to something fundamental in the human condition. Psycho-social maturity and competence among humans consists of the integration of two factors: *communion*, or the need to be included, connected and related; and *agency*, or the drive for independence, individuality, and self-fulfilment.'

Basically, Popenoe is saying that children need both roots and wings. They get roots from strong attachment in the early years to their mothers, and they get wings through the stretching, teaching and training of their fathers — the safe person who introduces them to the wider world. Mothers teach us to be grounded and secure, while fathers teach us to reach for the stars and stand on our own two feet in a hostile world!

Biologically — as we shall see in later chapters — boys are wired for competition, and revel in competitive, physical sports. These are tests of strength, skill and vigour that bring boys great joy and teach them many valuable life lessons.

We might need to be wary of universally applying 'girls' rules' (things that girls enjoy) to boys. There is growing evidence to show that boys do better in boys-only schools, because they value the simple rules, the mentoring type of leadership and the freedom of boyish expression.

Celia Lashlie, author of *He'll Be OK*, was initially concerned about the amount of physical contact she saw in boys' schools but, as her study continued, she realised that the jostling and physical jibing between the boys was actually friendly expression and all part of male bonding and friendship.

Best-selling Australian author Steve Biddulph makes the salient observation that there was a 400 percent improvement in boys' English scores when they were segregated from girls in classes. They were allowed, in a safe environment where they wouldn't feel stupid in front of the girls, to read and write poetry, act in plays and write essays about subjects that interested them.

> Giving boys labels for their emotions from a young age will lead them towards much richer lives and opportunities for greater intimacy.

Boys do actually have a rich emotional life, and we must work to protect it. The irony is that, in response to some of the extreme political correctness of the last few decades, a reactionary 'macho' culture has grown up among men and boys, glorifying the worst side of gang culture, video games and the media. This one-dimensional glorification of meanness, bullying and violence means that the emotional life of many boys is stunted, or displays itself in stoicism or the putting on of a 'mask'.

We, as parents, need to foil this demeaning culture by being aware of our sons' lack of instinctive ability to interpret their emotions, and by training them to understand themselves and analyse their feelings.

Giving boys labels for their emotions from a young age will lead them towards much richer lives and opportunities for greater intimacy, as well as providing them with tools to process the bad things that happen.

Our three-year-old grandson recently visited a fun park with his parents. When asked on the way home how he enjoyed it, he replied, 'I was happy when we went down the waterslide, but I was sad when I went under the water.'

He may have actually meant 'scared' rather than 'sad', but his attempt to label his feelings is a good start in the healthy process of interpreting what's going on in his emotional life.

Evidence suggests that men and boys tend not to be as insightful about their feelings as girls. Boys sometimes act 'unfeeling' in order to protect themselves, and if they are treated as unfeeling they will become even more so. They need us to coach them into understanding their feelings and help them to identify the underlying belief, or what they are telling themselves, that leads to those feelings.

We also need to give them support in dealing with negative peer culture and, when possible, to become part of a peer group that will positively change the way they behave and feel about themselves.

There are two particular strengths that will help you parent your boys. If you understand these, they will be your ally in your parenting journey. The first is that *if you give a boy a plan, he feels secure*. Not lots of detail or instructions, but a plan he can follow. And the second is that *he will be loyal to those who believe in him*. Believe in your son and he will thrive. Your respect for his ability and character will be food for his male soul.

IN SUMMARY 👁

HOW TO VALIDATE YOUR BOY'S MALENESS

Boys tend to explore the external world in a much more physical way than girls. They like things that excite their senses and gather information about the world by feeling, touching, poking or sniffing.

- They need opportunities to explore and investigate and discover how things work.
- They need to kick balls, run races, climb bars and pit themselves physically against a challenge.
- They need structure in their life and help with being organised.
- They need goals and coaching in how to be persistent.
- They need a safe environment and a zero-tolerance attitude towards ridicule.

Chapter 3

The importance of fathers

A father is someone who will play with you, even though he has friends of his own.

— seven-year-old boy

There's something about it when a man doesn't get along with his father. It makes him mean; it makes him dangerous; it makes him angry.

— Bill Glass, former NFL professional player,
after thirty-six years of prison work

Without male role-models, boy culture feels lost . . . Boy culture that is not mentored by spiritually vital elder males is more a gang than a culture. The elder males provide it with inter-generational magic, discipline, and direction.

— Michael Gurian, The Wonder of Boys

Every boy needs a male in his life, to help him 'download the software' of how to be a man. This is the greatest privilege given to a father, and the greatest gift that a father gives to his son. There is a special bond between fathers and sons, and joy for a boy in being approved of by his father. Testing his strength against dad and learning about life from this figure is a boy's best protection from life's worst scenarios, including violence and failure.

A father's guidance, instruction, encouragement and love are a child's connection to the world of men. Many studies over the last few decades have reinforced the observation that a father's role in a boy's life is crucial, as well as identifying the sad fact that when a dad is absent or angry, boys are badly disadvantaged.

Studies have shown that dads can never be too involved with their sons, and that this involvement has massive implications for the future. Well-fathered boys show the positive effects years later, by their capacity for empathy as well as by the health of their social relationships and capacity for intimacy. (Study by Robert Sears, Santa Clara University; Glueck Study, John Snarey at Harvard University, quoted in *Real Boys* by William Pollack, PhD.)

These studies show that boys whose dad is involved with them from a young age do better in every way. Academically they thrive; emotionally and socially they have the skills to cope, and their career success is influenced positively.

Unless there has been abuse, offence or neglect, every father is a hero to his little boy.

The greatest pleasure as a man, for me, has been parenting my sons and being involved in my grandsons' lives. The unexpected spin-off for me personally has been the opportunity to re-parent myself over the years. Working as a parenting team with my wife Mary, I have experienced a myriad of feelings, activities and family togetherness that have enriched my life and forced me to mature. Through friendship involving humour, challenging circumstances and celebrations with my boys, I have a rich memory bank full of mutual respect and admiration.

Fathers have a special way of relating to sons, which falls into the role commonly called 'male bonding'. It's the father who connects the boy to the wider world, with all its risks and thrills. I'm sure that it was me who first threw our baby son into the air. Mothers would never think of doing a silly thing like that. My little boy's eyes opened wide with fear, but his dad was smiling, so he was reassured. 'This is a new experience . . . It's different . . . but it must be all right because Dad is OK with it.'

It's a boy's dad who creates safety and reassurance when life feels scary, and who shows him what level of fear is OK.

> *My Dad represented the world beyond Mum. He would introduce me to strange things. Things that frightened me. But even though the 'thing' was unfamiliar, the experience was now very familiar: genuine fear, but the presence of my Dad meant that the risk was not too great. Fear followed by reassurance. He would hold me as huge waves (knee-height!) surged towards us. He would hold my fingers out for a calf to suck. He would row me across the totally alien environment of water. He would run with the pushchair, heave the swing up to shrieking height, and show me a flapping fish he had just caught, then gut it. All terrifying, especially if my Mum frowned and tried to intervene, but if Dad's holding your hand, it's safe and it's fun.*
>
> *He taught me that the best adventures and life's greatest treasures are very close to that edge of terror, and that courage unlocks life. There would be more lessons — about risk and caution — that life would take decades to teach me, but Dad taught the foundations.*
>
> *— John Cowan*

Fathers are not male mothers. They have a parenting style all of their own. A mother recently told me she had spent hours organising and preparing a birthday party for her three-year-old twin boys, and they had a great time. When they were tucked into bed that night, she asked what the best thing about their day had been. They both said, 'When Daddy bounced us into bed.' This wasn't about not appreciating or enjoying the birthday party; it was about the 'magic' of the 'daddy time' at the end of the day that celebrated their boyishness.

You see, the ways of playing with his son that come naturally to a father actually tend to be the very interactions that boys need. The physical play, often raucous, engaged in by a dad, and the tendency to push the boundaries, are very healthy and necessary components in the growth of a boy. Where mothers tend to nurture and soothe their children, fathers often 'rev them up' as it were, operating in their own special male way of playing with and teaching their sons.

It's what Harvard psychiatrist Jim Herzog calls 'kamikaze' play. William Pollack, in *Real Boys*, explains how research shows that such father play, or 'enthrallment', has many developmental benefits because it forces children — and this is especially significant for young boys — to learn to regulate and tolerate their feelings. 'A father's playful and vigorous type of play forces a boy to read his father's emotions.'

The rough-and-tumble, activity-orientated involvement with a dad that often drives mothers crazy is vital to a boy's development. These interactions, in an amazing way, teach him how to handle his aggression without fighting and with good communication. This is the reverse of what many would think.

The physical games are not just male craziness, but rather teach a boy many lessons, including how to monitor his emotions, how far to go and how much he can cope with. Simply, he learns how to 'read' dad, and how to listen to his own emotions. If a young boy ends up crying when the game goes too far, or opts out when he is not coping, then dad knows his son needs more support and help to handle the situation.

The boy is learning how to read dad's facial expressions and body language, and how to figure out where the line is for acceptable behaviour. This is part of helping a boy to master social encounters with other people. He is learning what it is like to experience a range of emotions that sometimes overwhelm him. He is learning whether dad is joking or is letting him know that he has crossed the line. A dad can measure the game so that the boy is not frustrated to levels he can't cope with, and talk him through and support him as he matures and develops emotional control.

I play a game with my grandsons in which I grab hold of them and hold them firmly, so that no matter how much they struggle and fight they cannot get out of my grip. When they start getting frustrated I say,

'What is the magic "password" for you to escape?'

The magic phrase is 'Grandma is a beautiful lady.' Seldom will these three- to six-year-olds come out with the 'password' the first time. They will struggle and make a variety of combinations of the password, by just changing one word, as they pit themselves against me not only physically but also mentally. They will struggle until they are exhausted, but both they and I know that there is the 'password', and that is the safety valve.

As another example, I have a friend with four sons. Each Thursday evening they have the 'worldwide wrestling championships'. The furniture is moved to one side, an old rubber mattress comes out and the fun begins. Every boy has to 'high-five' his dad with these words. 'It starts in laughter — it ends in tears — but it ain't going to be me!'

What a smart dad! This highlight of the week for his boys allows them to experience a type of male intimacy that is both pleasurable and a learning experience. Throughout their lives these boys, along with every other little boy, will pit their strength in competitive games and contests, and will be asking themselves if they are up to it. To learn the rules of playing with other males in a physical way, while keeping boundaries and rules intact, is important.

Father–son messages

William Pollack emphasises the life-long importance of early father–son lessons in emotional management. He says, 'They have been linked to later capacities in the boy to manage frustrations, explore novel circumstances, and persevere in academic problem-solving.'

Your love for your son will honour his questions about his acceptability in the world of men. Our subliminal and overt messages must always be, 'You've got what it takes, son!' We must make sure that we avoid sarcasm and the male tendency of using 'put-downs'.

If, as a child, we experienced constant verbal put-downs from our own fathers, we need to consciously practise new phrases. Think about what your boy needs to hear from you and practise it. It is the empowering language of 'You can do it . . . you're up to it'.

The good news is that you can turn parenting around in one generation. If you came from a rubbish family, you can be a great father. The clue will be to neither copy your own father nor just react against him and become passive. Tragically, many fathers who themselves had unreasonable, angry fathers become 'jellyfish' fathers to their own children, because they don't want their boys to experience the pain that they did. However, what a child needs is an 'effective' father — a backbone father — loving and firm, fair but friendly.

I have seen fathers use mocking put-downs of their sons, humiliating them in 'tests of strength', tragically losing the opportunity of getting across to the boy the message that he is capable of exercising both skill and honour to overcome the challenge. Public humiliation is toxic to a boy. He is longing for dignity and respect, and we must avoid ridicule in any form.

The power of male affirmation

In the children's movie *The Chronicles of Narnia: The Lion, the Witch and the Wardrobe*, based on the books by C.S. Lewis, there is a scene where Peter prepares for the final battle with the White Witch. As he stands apprehensively looking out over the assembled troops, his sister beside him whispers, 'Aslan believes you can do it.' Immediately the message finds a place in his male soul. Peter's shoulders go back and he stands taller as it dawns on him that Aslan trusts him to succeed. The younger brother, Edmund, because of Aslan's forgiveness for his selfishness and foolishness, which put the whole family in jeopardy, now also rises to the occasion.

Here an eternal truth is captured: young males rise to the occasion under the approval of men they respect. As fathers, we hold in our hands the opportunity to inspire our sons to achieve, offering support and modelling what it is to be a man.

These two instances show graphically the power of male mentoring for boys as they grow towards manhood. The belief in a boy's ability to succeed, as well as male support addressing problems when things go wrong, are two sides of the coin. When behavioural issues arise, or a boy fails, he needs to know that someone is there to show him how to get off the bench and back into the game again.

Dad — you can coach your son out of the hole he has dug

After a parenting seminar, a well-known sportsman rang me wanting advice. He had picked up heaps of useful advice, but he was still unsure about how to deal with a family conundrum. His six-year-old son had just kicked a hole in the wall after being sent to his room for 'time out'. This dad instinctively knew he had to take action, but his wife felt there could be 'deeper issues involved'.

However, little boys need immediate help to see a way forward. I suggested to the dad that he apply the principle of supporting the boy but also addressing the behaviour; that he stand with his son, looking at the hole, saying something like this: 'OK, we have a problem here with this hole. How are you going to solve it?'

In other words, tell your son that you know he has the mettle to come up with a plan to fix it. You know as a dad that he will need your guidance and help, but he needs to know that this is not acceptable behaviour, and that mum and dad aren't fazed by it. Dads often have to help their son to get out of the 'silly pit'.

> Give your son ownership of the problem and the tools to solve it, and leave his dignity intact.
>
> — *Barbara Coloroso*

The son in the example above may have come up with some creative ideas like 'Granddad will fix it', or 'I could fix it with the carpentry set I got for Christmas'. But eventually the dad and his son would have to come to an agreement. It may involve ringing Granddad, but must include some loss of pocket money and a real contribution by the boy to put right what he has done.

Your goal is to shake hands with this 'junior criminal' (just joking) after he has been through the process of ownership of the problem, restitution (fixing what he has done) and reconciliation (now the issue is forgotten). Many bad atmospheres and resentments smoulder on in families because parents do not have a process to deal with such behavioural issues, resolve them and then allow a son to move on.

Consistent love

An available father and an intact family are a significant protection factor for boys against involvement in crime. The unconditional and continuous love a father has for his son is vital. If love is conditional, it is not love — it is negotiation.

Bill Glass, a former NFL professional player who spent thirty-six years working with juveniles in prison, said in 2005, 'I was in a prison in Texas recently where there are 300 boys, aged ten to fifteen. These boys have committed every crime you can imagine. I asked the warden, "How many of these boys got a visit from their father in the past year?" "One," he said, "and he only stayed fifteen minutes, got into a fight with his son, and stomped out mad."

'They're not fathers, because fathers hang with their kids no matter what.'

Dr John Graham, writer of the foreword to this book and former principal of the largest boys' secondary school in New Zealand, told me that, in his experience, if a boy was in trouble and the father as well as the mother became actively involved in helping solve the problem with the school, then things got sorted out.

Dads, sport and boys

Everyone wants to belong and, for a boy, being part of a team makes him feel at home.

Sport has a special role in boys' lives. It is the 'virtual' battlefield and the opportunity for him to master a thousand disciplines, as well as to experience a singular sense of mastery and male bonding. It is an outlet for his physical-ness, and gives his competitiveness structure and discipline.

Very seldom will boys, even little boys, break up a game if they have an argument. They will usually return to the game and carry on — to boys, it is the *game* that's important. If little girls playing a game have a disagreement, usually for them the game is over. They will walk away or become upset. The *relationship* to them is the more important thing.

Well into their late teens and adulthood, many boys will continue to play sport, whether they are top players or just able to compete at an amateur level, because they enjoy the intimacy of the game. Boys and men enjoy the simplicity of the competition, and the camaraderie that follows as they talk over the moves and the goals.

One of the unique issues for our boys is their need to belong to a sincere community of men. As C. S. Lewis said very well in his book *The Four Loves*:

'In early communities, the cooperation of males as hunters or fighters was no less necessary than the begetting and rearing of children . . . Long before history began, we men have got together, apart from the women, and done things we had to and like doing. What must be done is a characteristic that has survival value. We not only had to do things, we had to talk about them.

'We had to plan the hunt and the battle. When they were over, we had to hold a post-mortem . . . we ridiculed or punished the cowards and bunglers, we praised the star performers . . . we talked "shop".

'In fact, we enjoyed one another's society greatly: we "braves", we "hunters", all bound together by shared skill, shared dangers and hardship, esoteric jokes.'

Even if your son is not a gifted sportsman, take him to sports games, explain the basic rules and coach him in ball skills, so that he can join in at an adequate level of competition with the other local boys. A boy needs to feel competent and accepted into the culture of 'boy games'. If he feels different or excluded at an early age from other boys and older males, he will absorb many negative messages about himself.

Boys tend to enjoy the 'tribal' experience. Being with a group takes away the pressure of too much one-on-one conversational and emotional intensity, and gives their male brain, with its fewer neural connections, time out to process. They thrive under affirmation from a variety of people, and they also tend to get that through sport.

During a recent conversation, New Zealand's Principal Youth Court Judge, Andrew Becroft, made two observations: the high number of male adolescents in trouble with the law in New Zealand who lack fathers, and the fact that, invariably, young male law breakers are not involved with sport. These two issues may be related.

Dads — sport is a great way to enjoy your son. Without driving him or taking the fun out of it, nothing will more greatly motivate even a little boy to finish his chores, eat his dinner or allow you to wash his hair than a promised game of cricket in the back garden or local park. You can introduce him to healthy sports activities and you can talk sport with your sons. As one teenage boy told me, 'for a while there Dad and I could hardly say two words to each other, but we could always go out and play cricket together in the backyard. It was safe common ground'.

When things are becoming tense at home, and discussion is getting heated, suggesting to your son a few baskets in the backyard or a run around the block can be just the pressure valve outlet that he needs.

Responsibility and the work ethic

Dads will push boys to experience the thrills that come from taking risks. They will also teach their sons responsibility and the work ethic.

I've a friend who runs one of the largest supermarkets in our city. He has amazing staff. Every one of his workers gets a job that involves responsibility — even the young boys with after-school jobs are included. That is so smart. He's giving the boys responsibility and expecting them to step up to the mark.

Boys need a sense of mission and belonging, so you need to give each of them a sense of being a vital member of the family team, a member who is significant, loved and valued for himself and his contribution. You are not doing your son a favour by making life easy for him, by not expecting any contribution to the family. His compliance in little things, including putting his clothes into the dirty washing hamper, or fulfilling his daily chores, such as feeding the family pet, bond him to the family and give him a sense of significance.

As fathers, along with our wives, we must put in place a sense of direction and mission for our family — clear guidelines around what your family stands for and values, such as loyalty, cooperation and hard work. Your boys will feel secure, honoured and part of 'the team'.

Father-and-son bonding

Stephen Biddulph, the Australian parenting expert, says that a boy at the age of four becomes a male-role-model-seeking missile. A boy at this age longs to be around men. Your 'dad' conversations and answers to his questions are all part of 'downloading the software' of how to be a man.

How does a dad entertain a small boy? By involving him. Take him with you when you go to the hardware store. Give him a task as you work together in the garden or your workshop. Then celebrate his accomplishment. Give him an errand to run or an important tool to hold. Get involved in something he is doing, like a project or a sport. Take an interest and show practical support. Invent your own story, with your son as the hero, and tell it to him when you are together.

For example, a friend who takes his school-age sons fishing is working on developing their skills. After a recent weekend of fishing he gave them a video on how to attach a hook correctly to the end of a fishing line, suggesting they watch it and then practise. He challenged them with, 'When I come home from work, you can show me what you can do!'

Involve your son in a male 'family tradition', such as making pancakes for the whole family for breakfast on a Sunday morning.

Shoulder to shoulder is the best way

Share your enjoyment of traditional male actvities. Boys love to learn about the world of men — cars, computers, fishing, woodworking, bushwalking.

Connect with your sons through story telling, just silent company or any shared activity; anything that they enjoy and you enjoy showing them. Your boy needs to know you in different moods and different activities — fixing things, driving in the car, cooking or reading together.

A boy learns compassion from his father

It is true that fathers don't always respond in the same way to a child that mothers do. However, recent research has shown that fathers respond with equal empathy to a crying baby as mothers do, but express their responses in a different way. In my experience, fathers feel tremendous love for their boys. This love may express itself in doing things for them, or just in providing. They want to protect their boys from cruelty at the hands of others.

Fathers that I speak to love their sons with all their hearts, and they want to be good fathers. However, a lack of male conversation with their own father, or the anger or negativity they experienced from him, may have left them with patterns of operating that fall short of the ideal.

It is not a weakness to ask for help to address your own issues of anger or 'flooding' when conflict arises — your love for your sons should be enough motivation. Think of the power you have to break a cycle and avoid inflicting the pain you experienced on your sons. As your boys see you address your issues they will not see it as a flaw in your character, but will admire you. And you will be giving them permission to address their own anger.

As a boy sees strength and kindness demonstrated, he will learn from his father a true model of manhood.

In *Life Without Father*, David Popenoe explains that 'it is a father's presence in a boy's life that encourages empathy and compassion. Those boys who spend significant quality time with their fathers (at least once or twice a week), such as during bathing or feeding, show higher levels of empathy and compassion.'

Other benefits of a dad's involvement

- The presence of a father helps children develop more links between the left and right side of the brain. Therefore boys especially have increased ability in speech when they have available fathers.
- Boys who spend quality time with their dads have higher ability in mathematics.
- Boys without fathers are four times more likely to drop out of school and many times more likely to end up as drug and alcohol abusers and delinquent.
- Incidence of mental illness is far lower when there is a father still in the home.
  — David Popenoe

Fathers and humour

Jon Gadsby, one of New Zealand's best-known comedians, tells how a guy came up to him and told him how well he remembered him. As a child, Thursday night (the night of Jon's television show *McPhail and Gadsby*) was the only night he was allowed to stay up, and it was also the only time he heard his father laugh.

Boys need fun, surprise, jokes and warmth from their dad, because fun creates a safe environment in which they can grow. You see, your boys won't remember all the details of your home life, but they will remember how it *felt*.

Men know the importance of humour and mutual admiration

Dads, if you've been working late, rush into your children's bedroom when you get home, get the boys out of bed and say, 'Quick, hop in the car.' They'll ask 'Why?' 'It doesn't matter — in the car!' 'Do we need to put on our clothes?' 'No, your pyjamas will do.'

The kids think, 'He's angry with us; he's taking us to the glue factory to melt us down!' Instead, Dad drives down to a takeaway and orders two thickshakes 'for the best players in my team'. He turns to the kids and says 'what flavours, guys?' 'Oh, banana.' 'Chocolate.' 'Right on,' says Dad. 'Make the third one strawberry.'

As they drive out with the thickshakes, the eldest child will usually say something like, 'Why did you do that, Dad?' 'Because you're in my team!'

Your kids know that you do crazy things with the people you love.

What if a boy has no dad, or a bad relationship with his father?

You've got to find a substitute father, someone who is committed to him, so that the boy gets the message, 'This man believes in me.' It may be not just one man, but a combination — a sports coach, a school teacher, grandparent, uncle or neighbour. In chapter 5, I give examples of mothers who have parented great boys without a father being present. These mothers have ensured that their boys are part of groups where men lead by example and are present in camping, club or team activities.

In fact, any situation where there is a good man present will enable a boy to create a template of manhood. Even a meal once a week with a family where the dad is present will be a great help, or where a man can read a story or play a board game with the boy. It's safe, unpressurised male time, and can lead to the communication of generational wisdom. There may be an elderly man in your street whom you know well and who would be happy to play a game of chess once a week with your son, or an older teenage son of a friend who would give him guitar lessons.

We, at parents Inc.,are experimenting with a programme, called the B-force, for boys who are growing up without a dad. In this programme boys who have no fathers can go once a month to a home and have a meal with a family who has a dad. Just by sitting around the table and observing the natural interactions of a dad in his family, even this regularly, is enough for the boy to 'download the software' as it were.

My observation has been that, although it would be ideal to ask two-parent families to take an interest in a boy who lacks a dad, it is not always realistic. With so many boys growing up in homes with only a mother and many two-parent families under financial and time pressure, it is not easy to ask families to take on the intensive responsibility of another boy. However, many families are prepared to invite a boy for a regular meal once a month.

These boys are gaining great value from the interaction in a two-parent family and gradually developing strong bonds with their hosts, as well as providing valuable 'time out' for their mums.

A family friend, a single mum with two boys, was grateful when her five-year-old son was invited to join family friends who live locally once a month for a meal. However, one evening when she went to pick up her boy, she collected not only her son but a broken stool as well.

It was explained to her that the father had been questioning the family on how a stool had ended up broken, and the five-year-old visitor had piped up, 'It's all right; I'll fix it.' The perceptive dad didn't dismiss this generous offer, but instead responded, 'Thank you Joshua. I appreciate that. I'll get it for you.'

Mum was a bit taken aback but, being a smart woman, she didn't complain, recognising the opportunity for Josh to shine. The next day she took her two little boys and the stool to the hardware shop and asked a 'tool man' sort of guy who was serving there for advice on how to mend it. They listened carefully, bought the glue and went home. The next day, for two hours, the little boys worked away in the garage, pulling the stool to pieces. Then, with their mum's help, they glued it back together — resulting in a repaired stool. 'You should have seen the look of accomplishment on my son's face when he went back the following week with the fixed stool,' she said. 'His chest swelled by several inches at the father's "Well done son — a good job!"'

Instinctively, that dad knew that little boys need the respect of adult men. And, where there is no father, mothers will need to take on that role in some part themselves, as we shall see in the chapter on the value of mothers.

Boys respond positively to leadership

I often tell the story of a Maori bus-driver driving tourists around New Zealand. He would come to a hill and point out how a battle occurred there between the British Imperial Forces and the Maori warriors defending their village — how ten Maori warriors had held up the British Imperial forces for six days so that their people could escape. Next day he came to a river and told how three Maori warriors had defeated twenty British troops. This went on day after day, until an American tourist eventually asked him, 'Excuse me, sir, but did the British Imperial Forces ever defeat the Maori warriors?' His answer was, 'Not while I'm driving this bus, lady!' This bus-driver was writing the script, and he was in charge!

Your boys will respond to your confident leadership. Be secure enough to take charge of *your* family. Have a plan. In this world that appears to be going crazy, how will you protect your sons from the worst excesses of our culture? How will you help them develop their own inner values and standards, and protect them from the world of drugs, alcohol dependence, pornography and sexual permissiveness? You will do this by setting the tone and creating a family where there is consistency, love, fun and communication.

The three Rs

Fathers are naturally wired to parent using the three Rs:
- Rules.
- Routines.
- Ridiculousness.

Rules

Every family needs rules, and it needs parents who know how to set them. Over the last few years I have had the privilege of speaking at a number of high school principals' conferences in Australia, and have shared with them the three questions Steve Biddulph suggests that all boys are asking:

- Who's in charge?
- What are the rules?
- Will the rules be enforced in a fair way?

At one such event, these questions stimulated great discussion at the mealtime following my talk. It was fascinating to hear the views of older, experienced principals who had used these guidelines and recognised their truth, and from younger heads of school who were realising the need to be simple, clear and consistent, and sometimes visual, with boys.

For eleven years now our organisation, Parents Inc., has conducted the Auckland Mayoral Fathers' Breakfast, attended by over 700 fathers. The speakers include CEOs, top sports coaches, business leaders and professionals. Every year I take the opportunity to run these questions past these leaders. Without exception, they passionately agree that these three guidelines are a universal basis for working with boys.

Routines

Structure is very important in a boy's life. His brain thinks that way, so he fits happily into a structured lifestyle.

The best start to the day for our family, when our children were young, was negotiated with my wife, who finds mornings a hard call. I am a 'lark', so the morning is my best time. Our family ran like clockwork when I went for a run, came home and made the breakfast, leaving my wife to make beds and coach the children in their morning routines.

We would all sit down together for breakfast, which often included a family reading followed by questions and a team talk. It gave us a great start to the day and meant that, by insisting the schoolbags had to be packed before breakfast, there was time for any last-minute emergency.

Routines take stress out of your boys', and your own, lives.

Ridiculousness

Don't neglect the fun, the edgy and the playful. Dads are great for pushing the boundaries and allowing boys to experience new dimensions of their life. Dad is the one who arranges the water-bomb fight with balloons full of water, and a big battle in the back garden. He's the one who shows the boys how to slide down grass hills in refrigerator boxes, and who plays their favourite character actors when they have a difficult job to do like cleaning their room.

If you are not a naturally funny guy, buy some riddle books and keep them near you during dinner time, to spice up the conversation.

Show love and respect for your boy's mother

A boy will get his view of women from the way his father treats his mother. Dad, your role is to be the strong and firm 'arm' who stands beside mum and backs her up in the family. There is a tonne of psychological power as two big people stand firm when there is family resistance.

Check in with mum when you arrive home. Kiss her first when you come in the door then, after you've played your ten-minute game with the children, tell them, 'Now it is Daddy's time to talk to Mum.'

A dad who teaches his son to respect women by honouring his wife, to respect his sister when she says 'no', and to monitor his speech, will offer a wonderful gift to future wives.

I remember a time when I was fourteen, doing the dishes with my mother. I challenged her, refusing to do as she asked. I thought my dad was in the lounge reading the paper. (I hadn't yet learned that dads can read the paper and monitor the family at the same time.) The next thing I knew, my father was standing beside me and saying, in his broad Scottish accent, 'You'll no' talk to your mother like that!' Strangely enough, I didn't ever talk to my mother like that again! His boundary of respect for Mum made a huge impression.

I would suggest that a modern dad uses a little bit more style, and says to his son something like 'Don't ever talk to your mother like that again. I searched the world for this woman. In fact, I evaluated thousands of women before I chose her. If there's ever a choice of who lives in this house, between you and her, it will always be her!'

ACTION LAB ⟳ TIPS FOR DADS

Daddy time

When you come home from work, tell your boys the game you are going to play during 'daddy time' after they have eaten their dinner. It could be 'the world-class river ride' (on a blanket), a story in the tent in the backyard, or a game of catch.

Wrestle relationships

Build physical touch into your interactions with your son.

- *A quick, unexpected grab.*
- *Hug and tickle.*
- *Pat and rub.*
- *Your own special way of carrying him to bed (a fireman hold, a commando hold, a gorilla hold, policeman hold etc).*
- *Wrestle and tussle.*

Be gentle and nurturing

- *Have your own Dad story that you tell your son each night, or have a tradition of a 'continuous story' around the dinner table. Everyone makes a contribution, even the littlest!*
- *Be comforting when necessary.*
- *Read books.*
- *Supervise homework and housework.*
- *Give him support when his emotions overwhelm him.*

Team parenting with other fathers

If you are a hunting, fishing dad then this is for you. A fathers' group in a country town has made this a yearly event, with prizes awarded at a dinner to round off the weekend.

The Big Three *(for teenage sons)*
With a group of other dads and sons, they meet on Friday night at 6pm.

They are organised into teams of three dads and sons. Within 24 hours each team has to catch three different sorts of animals, from deer to fish.

The Little Three (for younger sons)

As above, but they have to catch three different smaller sorts of animals. (Of course, the animals caught depend very much on the country you happen to live in)

Hikes and excursions

Plan a hike with your sons. Check that you have the equipment and sustenance you need, and set out. Begin the tradition with day rambles and then overnighters. Start when your sons are young and it will carry on, as something you do together when they grow older.

Games

- Monopoly and Battleship are board games that boys will enjoy playing because of their competitiveness. You can coach your sons in fair play and in following the rules.
- Hide and Seek, and variations such as Sardines. (In the Sardines version, one person hides and, once you have found them, you squash in with them until you are found by the next one, who then also squashes in with you.)

King Kong Game (from a family of four boys)

My grandsons have established a game called 'King Kong' that they love their dad to play with them. It's a pillow-fight game, where we put mattresses on the floor in the bedroom. It's a 'beat up Dad' game! The kids just say, 'Come on Dad!' and he walks into the ring, and they all attack him! The rules are that they can't kick, bite or punch anyone on the nose. They fight with pillows, bodies or blow-up toys! Sometimes the girls join in too!

Dangerous River Ride

Tell your sons that you are taking them on a river ride. Sit them on a *blanket and have them hold on tightly, then tell them there will be dangers that they have to negotiate, like waterfalls, and gorillas hiding that may throw things at them. Set up other members of the family with cushions to ambush them as they go past a door or couch, or to shake a blanket at them as they go through a waterfall.*

It sounds simple, but little boys love it.

IN SUMMARY 👁

WHAT BOYS NEED FROM A FATHER

Boys need a dad:

- Who is committed.
- Who will be a coach.
- Who is firm, fair and friendly.
- Who has a strong vision for his sons.
- Who can create fun moments.
- Who is consistent.
- Who will introduce them into the world of manhood.
- Who is prepared to break a cycle of anger or alcohol dependence.
- Who believes in them.
- Who will pass on 'adult wisdom'.
- Who will show them what to do and how to do it.
- Who will play with them.
- Who will give them traditions, and spirituality that will nurture their souls.

Chapter 4

The value of mothers

Our lives are shaped by those who love us and those who refuse to love us. Good mothering, then, involves far more than simply giving birth or providing a child with adequate physical care, quality clothes, a safe family car, the right stuff. It sometimes means standing against cultural pressure that devalues children. It may mean coming to terms with your own nurturing history.

— *Brenda Hunter*, The Power of Mother Love

A baby's mother becomes his secure base, or 'touchstone', allowing him to explore his world with confidence.

— *John Bowlby, British psychiatrist*, Attachment and Loss

A mother's love for her son and her instinct to nurture and protect him is the best compass she can follow in the early years. One of the ironies of modern life is that research is so widely available to us and that this research will often confirm what parents instinctively know. However, social agendas and politics can cause us to read research through our own world view 'prism' or set of glasses. It is not unusual for a mother to be pressured to ignore her natural instincts and her heart, for example, when peer pressure or financial pressures are pushing her back to work as soon as possible.

Your special place in his heart

There is much research that attaches high significance to a mother's physical presence in the first few years of her son's life. I want to encourage you to consider that, if you want to dedicate any window of your life to your son's welfare, the first two to three years should take priority. It is during your son's pre-verbal, precognitive years that his ability to trust, to feel good about himself and to grow a good brain are laid down, and you have a privileged role in that process.

Your child comes into the world with very few resources to survive on his own. You are the safe, warm wall between him and the world. Your comfort, touching, feeding and singing will sequence his brain and calm his emotions.

Later, boys do well and are stimulated by a group early-learning environment, and you will know when he is ready for this. Young babies, however, need 'one-on-one' responsive care. A baby doesn't see himself as separate from his mother until approximately eighteen months of age, when he begins to naturally break away. Every mother will recognise the burst of independence that comes with a two-year-old's language of 'no', 'me' and 'mine'. He is breaking away from you and establishing his own autonomy, while questioning how far he can go with that independence.

However, before that burst of independence, healthy attachment is important. In the first eighteen months of his life, everything is being laid down in his heart and head for future healthy, and even moral, living.

We have an epidemic of violence among men and boys and, although we are right to instigate ways for men and boys to control their aggression, we should also look deeper into how boys are nurtured in the early months and years. Rage, depression and lack of conscience can all be linked back to this early window.

Mothers not only nurture the character of children — they nurture their souls.

Our ability to shape our boys' conscience depends on the emotional bond we establish with them. If they have been given the comfort of our physical presence and consistently positive messages about their worth, then they will want to please us. In his book *The Moral Sense*, Stanford

University moralist James Q. Wilson wrote that conscience 'acquires its strongest development when those attachments are strongest'. And he added, 'People with the strongest consciences will not be those with the most powerfully repressed aggressiveness, but those with the most powerfully developed affiliation.' Wilson believes that a child's conscience is rooted in the soil of a warm, affectionate attachment with both parents, but particularly with the mother.

Simply put, because he is loved and learns to love in return, a child wants to please first his mother and then his father. Later, these attachments are 'expanded by the enlarged relationships of families and peers'. It is from this 'universal attachment' with each parent that a child develops a sense of empathy, fairness and self-control.

As a child is able to relax back into the care of his mother, knowing his own needs are met, he is able to build outward channels of empathy and conscience. Sadly, many psychologists and social commentators say that later depression, sadness, control issues and, in severe cases, chaotic thinking can be linked to an unavailable mother, or long periods away from a mother in the early months and years.

The pay-off for you

If we handle our babies with care and sensitivity in their early months, they will become sunny, happy boys who feel emotionally secure, and you will enjoy watching them mature into men who can love and trust. They will become happily independent adults, leaving you free to pursue your own interests and life. You are less likely to have to spend your latter years dealing with fall-out from their bad decisions and chaotic relationships. You will enjoy seeing them give this same nurture and respect to their own children, because they have the subconscious mental and emotional wiring and training they need.

Secure attachment to caregivers has been linked in memory research at Otago University in New Zealand with a child's early ability to show self-awareness and a better capacity to discuss personal memories. You will enjoy your little boy reminding you of the time you took him on the train and didn't have time to put his shoes on, or the time he threw his electronic Buzz Lightyear into your friend's swimming pool to 'rescue' the toy dolphin that had sunk, and you had to jump in and get it.

Mothers tell me that they do not always feel immediately close to their little boys. Some baby boys don't appear very cuddly, or as a tiny baby if he cries a lot, is colicky or especially needy, a mother can feel as if this is a totally self-sacrificing exercise. This is not unusual, and it doesn't mean you are not a good mother or that your needs are not important. Your needs are vital, and caring for yourself and getting whatever support you need should be paramount. Exercise and sunshine, sleep and good food, with a diet high in iron, plus the company of other women, really matter in this adjustment time. But you need to be reassured that the rewards will come.

You need to be reassured over and over again that what you are doing is valuable, important work for society. You need to be reminded that this time will pass, that you will recover your sleep and that, even though this may be a rough patch, you will fall in love with your little boy. It often takes six or seven months to really fall in love with your baby, and then mothers tend to describe it as the 'real deal' — a real love affair!

I remember the mother of twin boys, born eighteen months after her first boy, saying 'That first year was a total blur — but we laughed a lot. Sometimes my husband and I would just look at each other amidst the chaos and our sleeplessness and say, "Can you believe this!"'

No matter how blurred those early months feel, you have laid the foundations for a special place in your son's life, and you can be assured that those early bonds have set him up for a great future.

In the meantime, do get support, in whatever form you can, to get you through those first few months and years. It may mean postponing some financial goals and paying for home help, or just lowering your expectations as to what you can achieve for a little while, but your mental health is vital to your baby. You are his world, and the smile on your face will make him feel good about himself.

Look for friendship groups and force yourself to take part in anything that allows you to be with other women. Seek out your own mum, and ask your husband for support. Put a note on the door to stop visitors disturbing you, and sleep whenever possible when your baby sleeps. If you are feeling isolated, reach out for help. I would like all new mothers to know why they matter so much in the early years.

A mother's role in growing a good brain in her son

According to Dr Burton White's research at Harvard University, toddlers grew good brains when they had a mother who:

- Was loving, but firm with her discipline.
- Was available and open to interruptions to answer questions, give information and explain the world to him.
- Allowed full access to the house — allowing them to touch and experiment.

A boy's mother becomes a template for his future

There will be times in her little boy's development when a mother feels that her son seems interested only in 'blokes'. This will happen to various degrees over the course of his life, but you will always be a special source of wisdom and support.

My big, brave, outgoing grandson, at the age of four, is suddenly looking for 'mum reassurance' again. He recently unexpectedly cried because he wanted his mother to take him to kindergarten and stay with him. She was caught by surprise at his sudden need for her. But by 'listening' to him, she arranged to spend two days over the next two weeks as mother help at the kindergarten. Following this incident, he arrives at our place, with the compulsory finger-painting and the dirty knees, and I proceed with my grandfather tradition of making him a 'world-class hot chocolate'. As we drink it together I ask, 'What's the best thing that happened to you today, Sammy?' and he says, 'Mummy came as mother help to kindy again.' His world is re-secured for now.

Teenage boys and mothers

It will not only be toddler boys who need your reassurance and wisdom. Well into adolescence your son will look to you for maternal advice on how to live and how to relate, and he may need your support now more than ever. A teenage boy lives in two worlds — at home with his family, and in his outside social world, where often his friends wear 'masks' and he may feel the need to be 'on guard'. Make sure your home feels safe to him, a place he can unload, a haven where he is free to withdraw with his thoughts or to communicate his struggles. Physiologically, so much is happening in a teenager's body, and at the same time he is dealing with a society that is drowning in media, with large amounts of in-your-face violence and sexuality. Probably most of his friends' mothers are working and it is a time when he is making life-affecting decisions.

My wife Mary was always grateful that she was able to organise her day around mostly being home after school. She tells me how our sixteen-year-old son came home one day to find the house over-run, for the second week in a row, by toddlers and their mothers (the stragglers from a study group she had been hosting). He dropped his schoolbag, politely nodded to the company and withdrew to his room. Later, when everyone had left, trying not to sound ungenerous he said to her, 'Mum, do you think that group could be over by the time we get home? There's always things we need to talk to you about.'

Allow your boys opportunities to talk about how they feel. It may take a while for them to process what they actually are feeling, such as stressed or frustrated or sad. Learn to say things like 'Mmmmm . . . anything else? It sounds as if you are frustrated.' Or validate his observations with, 'That makes sense to me' or 'I can see how you'd feel that way.'

Let your boys know that emotions aren't right or wrong — they're just a signal of what's going on.

One mother I know has a code her family uses if they feel the need to talk. If she says, 'Do you need to talk?' and he says, 'Yes I think I need a 4,' she immediately knows that he needs a full-on opportunity to talk through a problem. If, however, he responds with a 1, 2 or 3, she knows that he'd like to talk, but it's nothing serious. She says it has been great for her boys, because they tend to have to sort through their feelings and decide why they are stressed or feeling angry.

There will be many challenges for mothers in this generation, living hectic lives and often finding themselves harried and stressed. However, after-school time should take priority. As Dr Phil says, 'We owe it to our kids to give them experiences, an environment and values that ensure that the feelings they experience at home are far more satisfying than any feelings they may get from drugs or alcohol . . . If we are to bring up a joyful child we have to spend the time with them and model a joyful life.'

Boys give their mothers the opportunity to enjoy adventure, surprises and great memories

Have you ever thought how much fun it would be to sleep on a mattress in front of the fire, or have a treasure hunt for your dinner outside? Your boys won't remember your untidy pot cupboard or the slightly neglected garden, but they will remember the things that made them laugh, as well as the excursions and adventures.

I had just finished packing up on the second evening of a parenting seminar in Sydney when a woman came up to me. She said, 'I've got to tell you what happened last night.' She recounted how she had bought my wife Mary's book *Cappuccino Moments for Mothers*, which encourages mothers to deliberately take a moment to plan a memory, or capitalise on a 'moment' to connect with their kids. She hadn't been able to put it down and had read it right through that evening.

The next day she came home, very tired after working two jobs, to find that her boy, with his young friend from next door, had dragged a pile of bricks on to their front lawn and built a fort. Her first reaction was to explode. But she'd just read *Cappuccino Moments for Mothers* and she thought perhaps there was something she could capitalise on here. This was one of those moments!

So she marched over to the neighbour's and said, 'Hey, lets make a bowl of popcorn and go and eat it with the boys in their fort!' She laughed, 'My neighbour, although tempted to take my temperature, agreed and within a few minutes we were both inside the fort sharing a popcorn party and some deep and meaningful conversation with our boys about their future careers as architects of the biggest tower block in Sydney!'

This mother, with a wry smile on her face, then told me, 'When I tucked him into bed that night my son said to me, "Mum, that was the best day I've ever had!"'

Mothers see the future through their children

It has been said, 'Educate a man and you educate a man. Educate a mother and you educate a family.'

Mothers have the great privilege of influencing the next generation of men. Mothers can respect themselves enough to expect respect from their boys. They can surround them with optimism, faith and a sense that they are capable. They can teach them the practical skills they need to survive and, especially, they can look for the goodness in them and expect the best of them.

At social events you often hear mothers talking about their sons. It is sometimes almost as if the mothers are vicariously living their lives through their boys' achievements. Don't get me wrong — every mother should rightly be proud of her son. But I hope that, in the end, the thing mothers are most proud of is the quality of their son's character and not just his achievements or personal wealth. There is a proverb which says, 'Happy is the man with a level-headed son; sad the mother of a rebel.'

The type of adult your son turns out to be will, in some way, be related to what you, their mother, value the most. That may sometimes mean valuing their character more than their comfort. In the long run, it is better to suffer the embarrassment of a son's misdemeanour and to make sure he takes responsibility for what he has done, giving him your support, than to gloss over it. The question Mary often asked herself about our sons was, 'Am I training them to stand for the "hard right" in situations where the "easy wrong" would be more convenient?'

Mothers' intuitiveness for their family

Women tend to be more concerned with values, and will often recognise an issue and instigate redirection in a family. Women are naturally more tuned-in to relationships and I encourage men: 'Remember, you sleep with a relationship expert. So listen to your wife, and if she expresses concern, ask her to tell you more!'

I have to confess that it was Mary who pushed relationship issues in our boys' development. I have always been thankful for the way she inspired us, as a family, to read a book and share in discussion with other members of the family over a meal. I remember on one occasion, at her instigation, we spent several weeks talking about friendships and their value. She had observed the different personalities of our children and felt that we could build on strengths and encourage them in areas where more balance was needed. Our eldest son was a very capable and focused kid, naturally more goal-oriented than people-focused. Mary recognised this and thought that, as a family, we should be helping all our children, and especially our sons, to nurture friendship skills.

She suggested that over the meal table we read *The Friendship Factor* by Dr Alan Loy McGinnies. Within a few months I noticed how my eldest son was becoming more proactive with friendships, initiating phone calls and suggesting a game of tennis or to go sailing with his buddies.

Now that he is a mature man I'm so impressed with how friendly and communicative he is with other people.

A mother's style

To some extent, mothers will have to go against their nature, which is more towards comforting and protecting, when they are parenting boys — especially if her husband is absent or they are parenting on their own. Because of a boy's need for simple and straightforward instructions and strong boundaries, you may need to toughen up, practise self-respect and what Mary calls 'stand on your pedestal inside'. I tell single mothers that if they want to know how to be a parent to boys, then a good start would be to rent a DVD of a Clint Eastward movie and practise the line, 'Make my day!'

With boys, you must be persistent and consistent. They must know that you are the boss and you must give up any hint of begging or pleading.

However, as they grow older, you must also gradually hand 'age-appropriate' control back to them. You must allow age-appropriate decisions, and give them plenty of practice at making choices — living with the outcomes of bad choices and learning from them.

There is more advice on age-appropriate decisions and choices in the chapters later in this book covering boys at their different ages.

Be simple and straightforward

Boys of any age don't tend to respond very well to long lectures and a lot of talk, or to their mother trying to explain how much they have hurt or embarrassed her. When it comes to discipline, you need to have a matter-of-fact approach, without emotion or manipulation. You act, after the first warning, and you follow through.

Be visual with boys. Set up family rules so they know where they are with you. Then when they misbehave, refer to the rules: 'Remember our family rules!'

An example of your rules for preschoolers might be the following:

Our family rules

- Do what Mummy and Daddy say, the first time.
- Be kind and thoughtful to everyone.
- Look everybody in the eye when they talk to you and always remember to smile.

HOT TIP ✔

For young boys, if necessary, use a behaviour chart (a rocket with magnetic stars, or a plane pulling along a kite (with squares to fill in). You can use this for short periods if your boy is stuck in a behaviour pattern and you want to help him change. It might be being rough with the cat, whining or refusing to greet people politely. Identify the positive behaviour you want — e.g. being gentle — and have a small reward when all the squares are filled in.

- Set up a behaviour chart like this to address a single issue. Emphasise the new behaviour you want, not the old one you are trying to move. Keep it going for no more than ten nights.
- Make it easy to change. Make the reward visual and the pay-off obvious, like a Matchbox car or a small toy sitting on the top shelf above the chart, or the promise of a trip to the pound shop when the chart is full.
- Work together with your husband to reinforce the message even more strongly. Talk about your boy's day after dinner, and whether he has earned a star today. Celebrate with lots of praise and positive attention. Remember, for little children a week is a long time.
- If he has had a bad day, and he doesn't get his star, tell him that tomorrow will be a better day. Little boys will not always get it right. This is a learning process. As one of my young grandsons says, 'Everyone has bad days!'

I overheard a delightful interchange between a young mother and her son in the supermarket the other day. The little boy was pushing around the trolley and singing, 'Twinkle, twinkle little bum, bum, bum, bum.' I was fascinated to observe his mother's response. She hardly reacted but, with a lot of style and still studying the tinned fruit on the shelves, she said, 'Oh Isaac, what a shame. You've got five gold stars on the fridge. Do you really want to lose them all for a black star?' The little boy looked at her thoughtfully for a second and then continued, 'Twinkle, twinkle little star . . .'

HOT TIP ✔

Have a simple way of dealing with bad behaviour:
- Send your son to sit on the 'thinking' stair or chair for two minutes (see below).
- Time out in the bedroom (number of minutes according to his age).
- Cooling off time (in their bedroom, the thinking chair, or in your lap).

If you are using a 'thinking' chair or stair, make it the same one every time. Use a timer. Your little boy must sit quietly and think about what he must do to fix what he just did. If he chooses to make a fuss or yell, the chair can be put in another room or outside on the patio, or you can put him in time out for two minutes. Hopefully, the neighbours will be understanding of a few minutes' noise — and they might just copy your parenting skills! After two minutes, bring him back to the family area to sit on the thinking chair. Tell him the timer doesn't go on until he is quiet.

Keep your nerve

A young family member was heard to say in a loud voice, as he was sitting on the thinking stair where he had been sent for two minutes to think, 'The kids at my kindy say you can't do this to me!' His mother responded as she continued with her chores, 'The kids at kindy aren't the boss. I am the boss,' and walked away.

Debriefing and restoring to the family

Occasionally, but not every time, debrief with your son, especially if he is upset. Cuddle him and talk about what got him into trouble and what will get him out.

'Why did you have to go into time out?' 'Because I was cheeky to Mummy.' 'Yes that's right — now what will you do next time Mummy wants you to put away the blocks?'

Or: 'Why did Mummy have to put the thinking chair outside on the patio?' 'Because I was kicking and screaming.' 'Yes, and what are you meant to do in the thinking chair?' 'Just think.' 'Yes — that's right — just think. Now, do you think that you could pick up those blocks and put them in the bucket? How about I help you get started?'

Helicopter parenting

Foster Cline and Jim Fay, the authors of *Parenting with Love and Logic*, tell how they worked in primary schools in low socio-economic areas where the boys showed a great deal of self-management. They got themselves to school, knew how to calculate the value of money and organise their own lunches. However, Cline and Fay also said that, in contrast, they taught boys in more privileged schools who forgot their lunches, expecting their mothers to deliver them, arrived late if mum didn't organise their morning and drop them at the school gate, and forgot their library books or gym gear.

Their conclusion was that school-age children are quite capable of taking responsibility for many things, including their own morning routines. It is parents who disempower them by continuing to make too many decisions for them, rescuing them from bad decisions and by generally over-functioning.

While acknowledging that our boys are still only children, we can encourage them to take on more responsibility with each year. Perhaps we will allow for one free delivery of lunch per term, or one rescue mission for something left behind, but after that the natural consequences kick in.

Mothers often worry about not being good parents, or feel guilty that they may be judged by others. However, you need to reassure yourself that your boys will not only respect you for having rules, but may actually be pleased that you don't embarrass them by arriving at school and handing over their lunch in front of their friends.

Later in this book, we will look at the type of family culture you can build to develop a sense of loyalty and belonging to your family. To be a great mother for boys you need to see how you can honour their need for simple rules, structure, a certain level of responsibility and a willingness to 'do a deal' with you.

Mothers and self-respect

Mary and I love our sons' openness, their energy and grittiness, their humour and sense of honour. However, Mary remembers how, quite early on as a young mother, she realised that she would have to toughen up in order to be the mother these strong boys needed.

Whenever our boys reminisce about their childhood their humour comes into its own. They often tell stories at our expense, and one of their favourites is the suggested scenario that as Mary lies on her death-bed breathing her final breath, she will lean over and hand over to her gathered children her most treasured possession — her 'job list' ! Our boys have also suggested that when she arrives in heaven, her first question will probably be to ask God why all the angels are standing around and why no one has given them a job to do.

You will gather from this little anecdote that Mary created an expectation in our boys that they would have responsibilities as part of our family. You will also gather that they were masters at gently caricaturing her family regime. However, the gratifying aspect is that because the boys knew there were good reasons for our family rules, and they also received plenty of appreciation for a job well done, there was always at least a modicum of healthy filial respect for their mother.

HOT TIP ✔

ARE YOU BEING BULLIED BY YOUR BOY?

It can happen in all sorts of ways; not only with physical violence. I heard a three-year-old say to his mother who had just corrected him, 'I don't love you any more.' The mother replied, 'Well, I still love you, Johnny; now let's talk about doing the right thing.' What a smart mum! She didn't buy into her three-year-old's reaction, but by ignoring it continued to teach him the right thing to do.

If you let your boy bully you, you will release big bullies into society. Deal with the bullying early; retain your self-respect, dignity and freedom as a parent.

Do not allow your boys to bully or blackmail you

If your boy doesn't respect you, your love may be wasted. It is love without boundaries, and is ineffectual in moulding his character.

I am reminded of a colleague from my years in youth work, who ran a home for 'at-risk' boys. He always said that, when dealing with delinquent boys, you have to win their respect before they will respond to your love. He said it was as if the more pain a boy was in, the more he needed to have the rules in place and the consequences of breaking them reinforced, before he began to sense any security.

I suggest to mothers that your boys receive the clear message that you are a leader who is not easily threatened. So if your son calls you a silly old bag (or something worse), instead of trying to get back at him through guilt by telling him about all the things you've ever done for him, just walk away. Don't try to engage or yell back; just withdraw your availability. Several hours later, when he comes to you asking, 'Hey Mum will you take me down to the shops, I need to get some stuff for school,' respond by saying something like this, 'I'm sorry . . . mothers do things like that — but "old bags" don't.' Don't, under any circumstances, take him. Always require some level of restitution and restoration for what he has done or said. Otherwise he will learn to use 'phoney' sorrys, which carry no level of regret or responsibility for the action.

A single mother told me that her eleven-year-old boy had called her a 'b . . . b . . .'. She had attended a seminar and remembered the above illustration. So she responded with, 'You will not use those words to me,' and walked away. She thought about how she could withdraw her services from her son.

The next morning she didn't provide his usual wake-up call, leaving him to take responsibility for his own morning routine. He got up in a panic, after sleeping in, as he had the responsibility of working the overhead projector at his school assembly that morning. He begged his mother to drive him to school, at which point she said, 'Mothers do things like that, but I' m sorry 'b . . . b . . . s' don't.'

He begged, pleaded . . . and even promised to do the dishes for a year! It was such a good offer, she said that she nearly took it up — but instead she remained firm. He had to walk to school. However, being a smart woman, she rang the deputy principal and told him what had happened. The deputy principal followed up by calling the boy into his office and asking why he had failed to be there in time to operate the overhead projector.

The boy fabricated a terrific story: a car had taken out a telegraph pole at the top of the street. Everyone was without electricity, and he had assisted the little old lady next door in her crisis . . . that had been why he was late. The deputy principal patiently listened, and then asked, 'Your reason for being late wasn't because you called your mother a disrespectful name, wasn't it?' The blood drained from the boy's face!

The mother is now the proud possessor of a note on school letterhead congratulating her on using tough love and a useful parenting skill — that of withdrawing resources.

Monitor the 'line of good taste' for your boys

I love the way my adult sons respect and honour their mother. Using humour and self-respect, a mother can be a tremendous ally through a boy's journey into adulthood. Boy culture can find itself easily sliding into the rude, the crude and the sleazy. Have rules about their bedroom walls — nothing lewd, crude or rude. In our family Mary would suggest, when a joke went too far, 'That story was below the line of good taste,' and after a lapse of judgement or a relaxing of a boundary she would say, 'Now — time to re-establish the line of good taste!'

When is a joke too crude? Or when is something not appropriate? Somehow fathers miss some of this. It could be just because we're blokes. But mothers have antennae that they need to use.

Although she had a great sense of humour, no one ever considered telling an off-colour joke or a sleazy story in my mother's presence. She had a way of raising herself to her full height of 4 foot 11 inches and asking, 'Is this a drawing-room joke?' Although it might sound quaint to us now, she was operating a very important principle for me and any other boys in the vicinity. In learning to respect her boundaries and values, we learned to respect all women.

Letting go

Mothers — you can have a strong vision for your boys. Let them know that you believe in them, and always expect the best of them, while giving them a lot of support.

Remember that you are preparing your son for adulthood. The strong foundations, the values and the words you leave in his head will equip him to make strong decisions on his own. And you can help him build an inner resilience through these sayings and wisdom.

When you are trying to avert your eyes from the 'gorilla's den' that your son calls a bedroom because you are waiting for him to fulfil the contract you have with him to sort it by the end of the day, think of his future flatmates, spouse or work colleagues. Make up your mind that you will not launch a son into the world who expects others to fix his messes.

If you ridicule your sons, or teach them powerlessness by doing things for them, you will sabotage their future.

Mary often used age-old wisdom to inspire or make a point with our boys. She wrote snippets of wisdom on the fridge, hung Rudyard Kipling's 'If' up in our hallway, and wrote a family prayer in their Bible. Our boys jokingly say those sayings messed up their lives, but in reality they gave them ideals to aspire to. Life-messages she handed on such as 'A good name is better than riches', and 'Your sign of greatness is your care for others', were her gift to them.

Mothers may find it really hard when, at some stage in her boy's life (usually after puberty), he gently pushes her away because he is establishing his own identity. At this point your son needs that distance. He has to decide if he will own the family's values, and he needs space to build relationships with other women. It is part of adolescence to seek greater autonomy, and you need to facilitate and work with this process, not fight it. Be proud of your son as he shows greater levels of responsibility and trust, and make sure he knows that the more trustworthy he is the more freedom you can allow.

A single mother, particularly, can find this breaking-away process painful as her boy, with whom she has had a very close relationship, launches out. However, if she does not cooperate and allow him the process towards independence, he may break away in a deliberately negative way, through drugs or alcohol, or just become highly unpleasant, angry and defiant. As I heard one expert call it, it's like the jilted lover syndrome.

It's important to know that a healthy process in your son's journey to manhood involves a time when he may not confide everything to you as he used to. If you are parenting on your own, he may want to go to live with his father. If his father is a good man, allow it. Much has been written about the need for teenage boys to be around good men, and Celia Lashlie articulates it well in *He'll Be OK*, when she says that, during adolescence, mothers need to draw back and allow the father or other healthy male role model to take him across the bridge to manhood.

This process is one to facilitate and enjoy. Once through the most oppositional years, you will continue to enjoy and be grateful for, if in a different form, the friendship with a great man whom you have had the privilege to nurture.

Read the chapters on parenting alone, and on parenting in adolescence, for more practical advice on letting go, positively and proudly.

ACTION LAB ⟳ TIPS FOR MUMS

Brighten up your son's morning

If you have a son who is hard to get out of bed, occasionally try a different approach. Explain that there will be regular special breakfasts and his favourite combinations, but no one will know on which day. This breakfast is only available in a ten-minute window. If he misses that window, then he has the 'regular' breakfast.

Turn special experiences into books he can read

Your small son will catch on to reading if you make books about those things he loves the most. Use your digital camera and photograph his outing with granddad, the day at the zoo, or his special camping night with dad. Buy an exercise book, paste in the pictures and write a story all about 'Reuben's Amazing Adventure with Granddad'.

Mum's tune-up

Everyone knows that engines need tune-ups. So do families. Have a tune-up family meeting if an issue has become out of control. Some parents call these 'family gripe' meetings. Everyone is allowed to bring one gripe, and the whole family must sort the issue out together. Everyone can suggest a way that it could be fixed. Then write down your plan of action in the family minute book. Boys love to solve problems.

Finish this meeting with everyone saying something positive about each person in the family.

Have a 'manners meal'

Warn the children that you are going to have a manners meal. They will be required to dress tidily, as if they were visiting someone else's house. Dim the lights, light candles, serve the food on large platters and pull out chairs for each child as they sit down. Tell them there will be a prize for the best manners at the end. Dad will judge. Make sure you have napkins, butter knives and more than one course.

Listening

Be a good sounding board — let your son run the challenges of his day past you. Listen, but don't forget to contribute your wisdom. You may save him from repeating mistakes. A good discipline is to learn to say 'Mmm . . . anything else?' before you jump in or express concerns at some revelation.

Create some focused attention with your son by making yourself available after school. If you are a working mum this may be while dinner is cooking, over a hot chocolate when you pick him up from a sports practice, or at the end of his bed at night.

Teenage boys can be the target of aggressive and precocious behaviour by some girls. Listen to his concerns about girls and peers, and give him some perspective. Encourage healthy friendships with a wide range of male and female friends and lots of energetic, outdoor activities to keep him busy, with valid excuses to fend off unwanted female attention.

Encourage him to treat girls as 'friends', not necessarily just as 'girls'.

IN SUMMARY 👁

WHAT BOYS NEED FROM A MOTHER

Boys need a mother:

- Who is available to talk and sing and play with him.
- Who respects herself.
- Who will expect the best of him and not the worst.
- Who will enable his sense of adventure and fun.
- Who envisions a great future for him.
- Who will be consistent and persistent with discipline.
- Who will monitor the lines of good taste for him and teach him to respect women.
- Who will listen to him.
- Who will allow him to take responsibility for himself.

- Who will expand his horizons in learning and creativity.
- Who will trust him with more freedom as he shows he is trustworthy.
- Who will launch him towards appropriate independence with her blessing.

Chapter 5

Parenting boys on your own

The woman who survives intact and happy must be at once tender and tough. She must have convinced herself, or be in the unending process of convincing herself, that she, her values and her choices are important.

— *Maya Angelou*

There will be many reading this book who are parenting on their own, and are perhaps dismayed to see the emphasis on both male and female role models. I can reassure you that single parents can and do raise great children.

I speak to hundreds of parents every year in this situation, and have huge respect for them; both for the load they carry and the resourcefulness they must sometimes call on to carry the double responsibility which, in a partnership situation, is shared. Often, I will suggest that if they are parenting on their own, the reason they are so tired is that they are doing the job of two people. Invariably I see moist eyes.

In New Zealand, one of our most respected rugby icons, Michael Jones, who is honoured not only because of his rugby skills but because of the moral, compassionate leader he is, was brought up by his mother. His father died when he was a small child, but his late mother made sure that he was involved with uncles, male coaches and a strong church community, and the results speak for themselves.

HOT TIP ✔

Don't allow your son to see himself as a victim. Many famous and wonderful leaders have come from single-parent backgrounds. We can grow up blaming our circumstances, or we can compensate by making good choices in our adult lives. Have dreams for your boys, and encourage them to have dreams for themselves.

One of my favourite books is *Gifted Hands* by Dr Ben Carson, an Afro-American who grew up in the slums of a large city. His mother was uneducated and cleaned people's houses to survive. As she was cleaning a house one day, she prayed that her boys wouldn't become members of the local street gang. A light came on in her head, and she realised that the houses of the educated and successful people for whom she cleaned had one thing in common — lots of books.

She went home and said to her two sons, Ben and his younger brother, eight and ten years of age, that they were to go to the library every Friday, take out a book and read it. They were then to write a report for her about the book. Her boys' whining response was, 'No other kid in my class has to do that,' to which she replied, 'You aren't no other kid — you're my kid!' (Don't you love her!)

Ben tells how, after a few months of this regular teaching, his teacher asked the class if anyone could spell the word 'agriculture'. Even though he saw himself as the dummy of the class, Ben noticed that none of the smart kids put up their hands, yet he could spell it. A few weeks later, the teacher held up a rock and asked what sort of rock it was, expecting the class to answer lava or volcanic rock. Ben put up his hand and said, 'It's obsidian, Sir.' He had just read a book about rocks. The teacher nearly fainted!

When he was fifteen, Ben realised that his mother couldn't read or write; she had just ticked his book reports in appropriate places. However, from these humble beginnings, Ben Carson grew up to be the first neurosurgeon at John Hopkins University to successfully separate Siamese twins joined at the head. From street kid to world-famous neurosurgeon — not bad parenting for a single mother!

The subject of single parenting is a book all of its own, but the key for parents on their own is to compensate for the parent who is absent by becoming more the way that parent needs to act. In other words, if you are a dad parenting on your own, you will need to be more nurturing sometimes than may be natural for you. If you are a mum, you will need to toughen up and be more simple and straightforward. There is a wealth of information in the other chapters in this book, and in the books I mention throughout (listed too at the back of the book), that will help you with raising positive, successful boys on your own.

Boundaries for mothers

Be wary of turning your son into his absent father. Mothers who turn to their sons for emotional support set up something very unhealthy in their relationship. As her son matures, and naturally looks beyond the home for friendships and romantic partners, the mother becomes a jilted lover rather than a valuable ally and coach. So, maintain boundaries around your role as a mother — do not burden your son with adult concerns, such as your finances and loneliness. It is your responsibility, as an adult, to develop supportive relationships with other adults to ensure your own emotional well-being.

There are many boys today growing up without their dad in the home. Unfortunately, if a boy's heart is closed to his father, he can be closed to all men. Your son does need to have a picture of his dad in his head. Boys carry around a picture in their head of their father, and that picture shapes their impression of themselves and men in general. Therefore, the more diverse, positive and realistic the picture is, the better a boy's perception of himself will be. Mum is usually the major source of information about dad, augmented with photos, stories from others and memorabilia. Make this information as positive and affirming as you can.

But mothers, be careful not to share more than you should about your own disappointments and bitterness.

Self-care

The major challenge of single parenting is finding any time at all for self-care. However, it is so important, and your children will suffer less through you taking some time away than if you burn out. Any support you are able to garner for this job you must take.

ACTION LAB ⟳ **TIPS FOR SINGLE PARENTS**

Capitalise on teamwork

Establish routines that empower your family and maximise the co-operation and fun a family can have. List jobs and let your boy choose. Make Friday night reward night. Celebrate the person of the week and allow him to choose the video or DVD you watch (within the family boundaries of course), the menu, etc.

Support and time out for you

Take stock of resources that are available in the community. Is there a relative or neighbour who can mind the children and give you regular time out (even an hour a week will be something to look forward to)? Can you establish a ritual of an hour at the library once a week after school, to give you quiet time while your boy looks through the section of his latest interest?

Trouble at school

All boys can get into trouble at school. Don't take it personally, or label your son as the 'naughty one', especially if you have another son who doesn't create waves. Work with the school to help him get back on track.

One mother told me that her disruptive son finally clicked that he

---

could be spoiling his own chances to be in a top sports team when she merely asked questions in a school interview. By asking about what would happen, but not overlaying it with any judgement or parental emotion, her son realised that he had to take charge of his own problem.

Give him space to be quiet

As a mother, you may feel that you know your son better than anyone, and you may want to always fix his problems or expect him to want to talk about everything. But, especially as he heads into adolescence, you need to give him space. 'Do you want to talk about it?' is an appropriate way of asking, and you must respect his answer if he says, 'No.'

Men and boys like to manage their own problems, and tend not to want to talk until they have a solution. As one mother said, 'It was amazing when I began to not pry. My son usually came back later and shared, when he was ready, of his own free will.'

Keep him busy after school

In several states in the US, there are large billboards on the highways saying, 'What is your child doing at 4pm?' The message is that it is not in the evening that boys get into trouble, but after school. One of our boys once said, 'You know, if parents can't be there after school, they should at least make sure that they have a dog to welcome the kids.' Coming home to an empty house can be a real downer. Try to arrange for an alternative if possible, even if your sons are teenagers.

HOT TIP ✔

Go back and read the sections on what boys need from fathers and from mothers in the previous sections. As a single parent, try to give your sons these same things *but don't forget yourself.* Ask for help from friends, family, neighbours or whoever — they can help you share the parenting load.

Chapter 6

Preschool years – the men your boys will become

How will I know how to behave, unless someone shows me? How will I know how to do things, unless someone involves me?

– Professor Richard Whitfield

I love preschool children . . . I love the way their minds work. I love the freshness with which they approach life. But a toddler can also be extremely frustrating.

He harbours a passion to kill things, spill things, crush things, flush things, and eat horrible things.

Tell me why it is a toddler will gag over a perfectly wonderful breakfast . . . but then he will enthusiastically drink from the dog's water and play in the toilet.

– Dr James Dobson

Remember the fire-engine cake your mother made you on your third birthday, or the special outing to the zoo when you were two when your dad carried you on his shoulders all afternoon? You may not remember all the details, but the collage of experiences will be imprinted in your mind. As a rule, not many memories survive from the kindergarten years and before that, just a murky amnesia — faded photos, shaky home videos and the anecdotes of others are all we have. However, it was in those mostly forgotten years that we learned to walk and talk and acquire most of the skills we now use every day. Most of all, this was when we learned to trust; when we made decisions about the world; whether it was a scary place or a place where the big people could be trusted to meet our needs and protect us from stuff we could not handle; and when we were introduced to the outside world at an age-appropriate pace. It was when the foundations were laid for every relationship we experience.

A few short years

Study after study shows how crucial those years are to every aspect of future development. During these years our parents are the centre of our universe. Our parents probably wondered at the time if all the things they did for us were worth the trouble. You probably sometimes wonder the same, as you struggle to cope with your preschool son! I want to encourage you that the effort is worth it. Though your son may never recall what you are doing for him, he will benefit from your nurture and care for the rest of his life. Parenting is the most important task you will ever do, and the consensus among child experts is that the secret of raising confident, loving and happy boys is developing strong early parent–child bonds. Our relationship with our young son opens the door to the rest of his life.

Every child is subconsciously asking the question, 'Am I welcome in the world? Is there a rainbow of promise around me not to be wounded or rejected?' The science is very clear that the early experiences of children programme their lives in a hugely significant way. A predictable, loving environment in the first few months of his life provides a foundation for all future learning and emotional memory.

> Children who don't play much, or who are rarely touched, develop brains 20 to 30 percent smaller than normal for their age.
>
> — *Baylor College of Medicine*, Time

Your son's brain goes through almost explosive development in the early years. Failing to provide adequate stimulation and nurture in these crucial stages robs him of future potential. Intellectually and, more importantly, emotionally your son will probably never be able to completely compensate or catch up if neglected at this stage. Eye contact, cuddling, singing and talking to a baby and toddler are crucial in the establishment of neural circuits that last a lifetime. Children who are not nurtured or stimulated lose synaptic connections, so that later in life the brain hardware is just not there. They become unattached, emotionally empty children, less capable of empathy and lower in intelligence. The 'brain-building' role is yours. It can be shared, but it cannot be delegated.

Dr Bruce Perry, an expert in brain science in young children, believes we can lose the cultural DNA of a society within one generation if we fail to grasp the importance of this. Every new experience is threatening to a baby, and it is the soothing, the touching, singing and loving from us that actually finishes forming the structure of his brain. It develops a sense of security and, later, his ability to hand on that emotional caring to his own children. Being either physically or emotionally absent from him at this time can have profound effects.

Family therapists so often find themselves dealing with irrational feelings of abandonment, powerlessness and phobias rooted in those precognitive years. The media loves to sensationalise angry young men, sexual addictions, road rage and so on and, as a society, we are concerned about boys who act in uncontrolled ways. But if we are to address these issues we must take seriously how we nurture our baby boys. We must also take charge and refuse to allow their neurological systems to become overloaded, through stress from abandonment or neglect. Neglect may not be physical, but it may be leaving him in front of the TV for hours, allowing scary adult images into your home or leaving him in his cot for hours on end, without positive eye contact and loving interaction.

The challenges for parents of preschool boys

Because of the structure of their brains, preschool boys may be more challenging for their parents than their sisters, who will often sit at one activity or with a book for a long period of time. It is true that young boys suffer more injuries than girls, because generally they are more adventurous. Small boys tend to be more impulsive, to be risk takers and explorers. Boys tend to be physically stronger and have abundant, exuberant energy. They tend to be noisier and messier.

Baby boys will often be attracted to mechanical movements and things that work, rather than faces. Their language may be limited to more 'motor noises' than words. In fact, it has been estimated that almost all the sounds that little girls make as they are learning to talk are conversational, but only about 40 percent of boys' sounds are language. The rest are his experiments with 'noises'!

As the parent of a young son, you may find yourself feeling challenged. As one mother joked, 'I have learned "stuff" through having boys. I have learned that a waterbed holds enough water to cover a 200-square-metre house five centimetres deep! . . . I have learned that a ceiling fan is not strong enough to hold a 21-kilogram boy dressed in Superman underwear and Batman cape, and I have learned that when you hear the toilet flush and the words "Uh, oh" then it's already too late!'

The golden rules for parenting boys

Keep it fun . . . Keep it calm . . . Keep your perspective.

Baby boys' brains differ from girls'

Many studies and books are available which detail the way that testosterone affects the male foetus in the womb and sets him up with certain characteristics. At six or seven weeks after conception, a chemical bath begins to masculinise the tiny foetal brain and alters the corpus callosum, which is the rope of nerve fibres connecting the two hemispheres of the brain. This process actually limits the number of electrical transmissions that can flow from one side of the brain to the other. It sets him up to have a more compartmentalised brain and less innate ability to be in touch with his emotions. This will affect him for the rest of his life. Whereas girls and women tend to be able to immediately access their feelings, boys and men will have to work hard to decide what they feel, and why.

> Whereas girls and women tend to be able to immediately access their feelings, boys and men will have to work hard to decide what they feel, and why.

The other effect that this flood of testosterone has in the prenatal period is the localisation of language development. For a right-handed man it is isolated largely in the left hemisphere of his brain, but for a woman it is distributed over both sides. I have stuttered from the age of six, and some specialists have theorised that being changed from a left-hander to a right-hander when I went to school, linked with other traumas, caused the confusion in my speech. Several other boy stutterers were linked to my first primary school teacher.

The extra testosterone and the lower levels of serotonin (a calming chemical) mean that, from the start, the aggression little boys show is more obvious. Boys' brains are more spatial, as they tend to operate more in the right side of their brain. Boys tend to use up more space with their play, as they build towers with blocks that are taller and higher than girls'. They will be less attentive and appear not to hear you as easily as their sisters.

Even if your boys are not at the extreme end of the testosterone scale, there will be issues specific to boys that you will discover as you are parenting your toddler. You may have to deliberately take your young boys out and allow them to run off energy; to take them to the park, the beach or the zoo more often. Yes, there will always be dishes and washing to do, but there will also be great excuses to leave the chores while you play a five-minute game of hide and seek, or take the picnic out to the fort they have just built. Enjoy your child during these years.

Phil Da Silva's twenty-one-year Otago University study emphasised that the most important three components for building a good life were really very simple. They were that the early experience of a child was rich; that care was consistent and predictable; and that children were loved.

The last few years have been a delight as Mary and I have watched five little grandsons grow through their preschool years. What grandparents can contribute to their children's parenting journey is perspective. We can honestly say 'It is just a stage'; or that most three-year-olds have tremendous imaginations and having an imaginary friend who gets blamed for misdemeanours does not mean your son is a pathological liar; or that a two-year-old's oppositional behaviour is normal and that your child is needing you to take charge and show him where the boundaries are. Yes, some children throw 'googlies' at their parents that are new variations on themes, but very often grandparents have seen it before at that particular age or stage. For instance, in the supermarket, it is very easy to pick the two-year-olds. They are likely to be the toddlers demanding, 'No!', 'Me do it!', 'Mine!' or throwing themselves on the ground to the embarrassment of their mother.

As grandparents, we are still enjoying the memory of Christmas Day last year when four little boys, aged between one and five, arrived at our house for Christmas dinner, in their best clothes, each clutching a new toy from Santa along with presents for their young cousins. The treasure hunt and the family concert after dinner are memories we will always recall with a smile. Each little boy, after a personalised introduction, was cheered and clapped before he performed his item.

Two-year-old Jonty, full of personality and charm, discovered the 'stage' that day. Having caught on to the fact that an introduction received big applause, he reintroduced himself between every item. 'I Jonty and I two and a half!' He joined in as support group to his big brother's rendition of *Scooby Doo*, and took centre stage whenever there was a pause in the proceedings. These four little boys all have unique personality quirks and gifts that give them a special place in our hearts. The confident five-year-old who kicked off the proceedings, or the impulsive three-and-a-half-year-old with the big heart and the 'all-in' personality who said his verses in his underpants because he had jumped into the neighbour's spa pool, thinking it was a trampoline. Not to mention the dear little one-year-old watching it all from the safety of my knee.

Practical parenting in the early years

Among findings from Dr Burton White's ten-year Harvard research programme on what built good minds in young children were the conclusions that the best parents excelled at the following three key functions:

- They were superb organisers and designers of their child's environment.
- They permitted short, focused interruptions so they could comfort, convey information and answer questions.
- They were firm in discipline while simultaneously showing great affection.

Fortunately you don't need a PhD in child psychology to bring up your son — just the assurance that the baselines are simple.

HOT TIP ✔

THE UNITED APPROACH – WORK AS A TEAM

Parents — it is essential that you stand beside each other, both physically and mentally, when you are parenting. Children are very good at sniffing out differing standards in their parents. Differing standards create insecurity and allow children to become sneaky or manipulative.

When parents stand up for each other, speak well of each other and check in with each other over parenting matters the children get a secure message: 'We love you and we are working on behalf of you.'

ACTION LAB ⟳ PARENTS OF PRESCHOOLERS

- Establish predictable routines and structure in your home. Routines are your friend, and will become your son's friend too.
- Decide what your family rules and limits will be. Children aged two to five should know how to:
  - *Do what mummy and daddy tell them to do.*
  - *Speak pleasantly to people.*
  - *Not kick, bite, push or hurt others.*

Managing a young child is a hands-on activity. Toddler boys have few internal controls. They are directed by impulse. If their newest skill is to climb, they will try to climb anything in reach. Toddlers are like the famous battery commercial — they keep going and going and going . . . They have an insatiable need to explore and will cut a wide swathe through the house, touching, pulling and emptying things. As a parent you should have realistic expectations; your role is to direct their boundless energy into acceptable channels.

Up to two years of age, boys are learning through exploration and experimentation. They are developing the building blocks of initiative, creativity, curiosity and autonomy. That is why it is important to allow safe access to a whole variety of touching, tasting and listening experiences. Allow him to splash in water, to feel a fluffy chicken, to bang the pot lids and to knock over the pile of blocks. Give him permission to explore and experiment, but don't neglect to be in charge. Be the 'gentle giant', redirecting him where needed. As you 'scoop and swoop him' from an out-of-bounds activity to one you permit, talk to him, even if he is non-verbal. Let your toddler boy know that the coffee table is not for banging on, that it is glass and will break.

Establish routines but don't sweat the small stuff

Remember that the touching, feeling, discovering process is an essential part of a toddler's development. Do not come down too 'heavy' or try to discipline your under-two-year-old for his natural inquisitiveness. Allow him to play freely when you can manage it.

Your goal is to gradually progress him from going straight from feeling to acting, to the more mature process of feeling to *thinking* then acting. This is a life-time project, but you need to begin addressing his thinking process when he is about two years of age. You will know when it is time to do this: when he begins to say 'No' and to show you that he is breaking away, beginning autonomy.

Tantrums, biting or hitting from an under-two-year-old should be handled by immediate 'time out' in their cot. Don't even make eye contact or engage with your son. Just swoop him into his cot, with as little emotion as possible, and say, 'No Matty (or whatever his name is) — no tantrums.' Leave him there for a minute and then go in and say, 'Good boy, no more tantrums — now come and play nicely.'

Functional behaviour: I feel — I think — I act.

Dysfunctional behaviour: I feel — I act.

HOT TIP ✔

PRESS 'PLAY'

Running around *after* your kids isn't the same as running around *with* your kids. Don't forget to occasionally press 'pause' and then 'play' and spend some wonderful time just playing with your children. Your children are going to remember the 'play' part of their lives more than anything else.

Get down on the floor with them, make huts out of blankets, have a water fight or a tea party, and see if you can find that board game to play after dinner.

Plan his environment

Plan his environment with some structured activity. A sandpit in the back garden, if possible, is a must for boys (or a large plastic container on the patio filled with sand), and things to climb or ride on. Set up outdoor activities in the summer: bubbles in the paddling pool; give him a bucket of water, add some food colouring and a paintbrush to paint the house; invite a child over who is your boy's age and let them run through the sprinkler in your garden; have chalk for writing on the path. Acquire cardboard boxes — they make great trains, houses or boats. Take five minutes to throw or bat a ball to him.

HOT TIP ✔

A child's own kitchen drawer
Keep a drawer that is easy for your toddler to open and close. In it keep plastic containers and tops, or anything else he is allowed to play with.

A rainy-day chest
Fill with inexpensive games and toys. Wrap each one in bright paper.

Book basket
Recycle books, a few at a time, bringing favourite and fresh ones out regularly.

Letter box
Paint a box to resemble a letter box and have piles of cards with animals and objects on them. Get your son to name them as you 'post' them.

Whenever possible, take your son with you on errands. Give him a task; real tasks are often more fun for boys than playing. Housework, gardening, woodworking. Let your boy stand on a chair beside you and 'help' and he will be in toddler heaven.

Plan outings. A ride on a steam train, a swimming lesson, a trip to the beach or to feed the ducks. Keep him busy, then coming home will be an event.

Begin the routine towards bed at 4pm. Have a tidy up, involving your child. Use boxes labelled with digital photos, and do it together. Play a favourite song and see if he can do it before the song finishes. Put him in the bath to wind down for the end of the day.

Have things for your son to look forward to like 'Daddy time', after tea, when you play games. Throw balls in a rubbish bin or whatever. Enjoy being a kid again.

Short is often very sweet and uncomplicated, as in a thirty-second, 'I'm going to get you', or 'I'll chase you to bed', or 'Let's see who is fastest at putting away our shoes!'

Try to observe your child, and listen to him closely at least three times a day. You will quickly want to stop and play — before he changes.

HOT TIP ✔

LOVE IS SPELT T.I.M.E.

Take ten minutes a day just to spend time with your child, enjoying them and watching what they are doing. Call it your 'special playtime'. Watch them, describe out loud what they are doing, follow their lead and give them your full attention.

Children love to feel you are attending to them. It touches their deepest need for significance and love.

More time together equals less time managing misbehaviour.

Comfort, answer questions and convey information

Your boy's personality

Many parents observe two types of little boys. The ones who are 'out there', very physical, adventurers and explorers, into everything with little fear. And then there are other sons who are more cautious, and more likely to stay close to their parent for reassurance and permission. It can be a rude shock when your first boy is compliant, then a second or third is high-powered, 'out there', confrontational or just plain tricky. Research tells us that 40 percent of children will be easy, 10 percent will be exceptionally difficult and 50 percent will be in between. Statistically, boys tend to have more developmental problems.

According to child temperament experts, we are born with a certain basic temperament and sensitivity to our environment. Some children are 'intense' and appear to overreact to their environments, such as sounds, touch, taste, smells and the feel of certain clothes. Some are entertainers, with sunny natures; others love order, and others have the sort of personality that loves to control and be in charge. However, this innate temperament will be modified by the content and style of your parenting.

HOT TIP ✔

Don't fall into the trap of blaming yourself for everything your child says and does. It is not what our children do, but how we handle the situations as they arise that is important. If we handle situations in structured, patterned and consistent ways then it will result in positive changes we want to see in our boys. And be proud of their strengths.

In my family, and among my grandsons, there are several 'A-type' personalities. They have wonderful senses of humour and big personalities and I'm sure they will be great future leaders, but as preschoolers they sometimes display 'lion-type' behaviour, wanting to be the boss or in charge. As the grandfather, I sometimes feel that I am part of their staff! They know how things should be and are definite about them. For instance, if we're playing aeroplanes, I'm certainly not the pilot. At our family holiday home, we have an old sailing dinghy set into the sandpit. It has a makeshift sail so the grandsons can play their 'pirate' games and just enjoy messing about in a boat. Sam's little friend was due to visit and he had been 'primed' that when George came they were both to be captains! No one was to be in charge. They could take turns. Young Sam had happily accepted that.

However, thinking I was doing him a favour, I had installed a pulley for the mainsheet, so one of them could work the tiller and the other the sail. I finished this just before dinner, but three-year-old Sam wasn't happy. I guess the mainsheet pulley was new and he wasn't confident with it and didn't want it there when George arrived. He asked if I would remove it, which reluctantly I agreed to do. However, Grandma decided that she could talk Sam into keeping the pulley. We watched from a reasonable distance as Grandma discussed it with young Sam in the boat. Jokingly, we discussed how the two A-type personalities would sort this out. To her credit, Grandma did very well, but Sammy wouldn't budge — until she used the very clever line, 'But Sammy, I'm a crew member. Crew members help sail boats.' To which Sam replied, 'No Grandma. You're a passenger!'

I have since used Sam's statement on Grandma when she's been negotiating with me, but somehow it never has the same effect! I have since convinced Sam that Grandma is the Admiral, but I don't think he understands what an Admiral is!

What I'm saying here is that it wasn't necessary to crush his spirit by forcing him to keep the pulley until he was happy. It is OK to negotiate on the unimportant stuff. Strong-willed boys can be strong-willed, but they can be sensitive at the same time. And there are times when we need to deal with the strong will and there are times we need to deal with the sensitivity, and that's the skill of being a good parent.

Be firm while showing great affection

Some parents despair over the behaviour of their young son, convinced that he has got something wrong with him or a syndrome of some sort. They usually wonder about ADD or ADHD. We certainly should be very careful in diagnosing these conditions. It is amazing how a young boy can seem super 'hyper' at two or three but when he later gets into a structured kindy environment, sport, gym or swimming, he becomes a totally different child; his excess energy is directed appropriately. Although these conditions exist (*Understanding ADHD* by Dr Christopher Green is a good source of information to begin with), they tend to be over-diagnosed. Dr Michael Gurian (author of *The Good Son*) believes that these boys are mostly just young Huckleberry Finns whose environments need to be modified to have a lot less electronic stimulation, and more calm routines and outdoor activities. There is no doubt that there is good science to back up the theory that some children have a sensitivity to certain chemicals in food, which creates extreme behaviour (some of these are naturally occurring chemicals). If you are concerned, you can research this topic. There are many good books, websites and support groups.

Discipline

> The basic tools of discipline come from knowing your child and helping him feel right. A child who feels right, acts right. Because you take the time to get to know your child well, he trusts and respects you and will be easier to discipline. The long-term benefit of this approach to discipline is that the groundwork you lay when your child is a baby and that you reinforce during his toddler years, will pay off during his childhood.
>
> **— William Sears, MD**

According to Kay Kuzma, author of *Building Your Child's Character From the Inside Out*, the influence of parents is a powerful tool in building a child's internal code. Kuzma says two key ways we influence our children are through our *expectations* and our *words*.

I am a keen observer of our grandchildren, with their varied personalities, and watch with admiration as our three-year-old is asked by his parents to think about 'the right thing to do'. An outgoing leader, this little boy's courage and impulsivity is often a source of frustration for his parents. Yet his response, 'Mummy, I *do* want to do the right thing,' when he's in trouble yet again, shows that he is learning to understand not just that his behaviour was wrong, but where the 'tracks' are for appropriate actions and words.

Discipline should be aimed towards helping your son think about the consequences of his behaviour and to make the right choices next time.

HOT TIP ✔

DEALING WITH THE STRONG-WILLED BOY

A small boy who is ruling the family with tyranny is a very insecure child. He looks at the family and thinks 'If I'm the most powerful person in this family, who will look after me if I'm in trouble?' For a three-year-old, that's frightening! Parents of boys need to be the big people and expect compliance. Compliance in the little things is the key to cooperation in the big things.

However, strong-willed children do need some area of control – so 'do a deal' with him and give him something to be in charge of.

I was approached on the second evening of a seminar by the mother of a four-year-old boy. She was parenting on her own, and wanted to tell me how she had tried a different way of disciplining her son after the previous evening's session. She confessed that her usual mode of responding when her son had messed up was to yell at him. But things had panned out very differently that afternoon, when she took a different approach. She had come home from work with my words from the evening before ringing in her ears. I had said that our boys need the message that 'they've got what it takes', and that we need to support them as they fix what they have done, not label them as naughty. I had said that we can give even our small sons ownership of their own problem and stand beside them as they find a solution.

This woman had come home with a large amount of groceries and, while she was putting it away, her small son went into the garage and hauled out a pot of paint that the painters had left behind from work on her fence. He took it outside and painted the side of the house. She was furious when she saw what he had done. She was about to go into her usual mode of yelling; however, she mentally took a step back and decided to try a different approach. She said to him, 'Whoa, you've got a problem here, son. This is not the paint for the house. What are you going to do about this mess? I know that you have got what it takes to fix it. You had better sit on the step and think about what you can do.' Within a few seconds he said, 'Mummy, I'm really sorry. I could get a cloth and some water and wash it off.'

She told me that together they washed down the wall of the house with warm, soapy water. They actually had fun doing it together and her son was so proud when he finished. She was able to say, 'Well done, son — I knew you were up to it!' and they were able to celebrate his 'putting it right' together.

HOT TIP ✔

SAYING 'NO' IS SOMETIMES IMPORTANT

In our permissive society, son-rearing is often focused on positive discipline and positive parenting.

I have no problem with this, but it is also important your son hears the word 'No'.

'No, you do *not* hit the cat; no, you do *not* hit your little brother.' A firm 'No' with an explanation is the beginning of learning right and wrong. Let him know he can do the right thing because it's the right thing to do.

'Stand and think'

By the time a child is two, he is ready to learn to think about other people, and about the social contract by which we all get along in the wider world. This social contract is about tempering our behaviour so that we can get along with others.

Your son must learn that:

- Other people have thoughts and feelings about what we do.
- We must think and feel about others before we do something.

Two years of age is an appropriate time to introduce 'the corner' as a discipline strategy — or 'stand and think', as some people like to call it. This is more than a 'time out' technique. It is designed to train your child to think and solve problems. When he has misbehaved or refused to follow a clearly understood direction, have him stand in a corner of the room. He is to stand and think about what he needs to do. A boy may need to be physically calmed and gently held in the corner if he is new to this family rule. After the corner has been used in your family a few times, your son will learn that resistance is pointless, and he will go and stand in the corner when directed to.

After a short cooling-off time, ask your boy, 'What do you have to do to get out of the corner?' If he fails to answer, or fights and kicks, keep him in the corner. He will eventually solve his own problem: 'I've got to pick up my toys', or 'I've got to play nicely with Ben and say sorry for hitting'.

A child's concept of time works in your favour. One minute in a corner is a long time for a preschooler, five minutes is an eternity. Even the most stubborn child will not last ten minutes before he agrees to the answer that will get him out of the corner.

This method is non-violent, it is transportable and can be used in public. He is not being banished from your presence, and any panic is brought under control by the calmness of the parent. It helps your boy to re-sequence his thinking and focus on solving the problem. Antagonism gets directed towards the problem, as you remain his ally while he works on it.

Remember you are doing this *for* your son, not *to* him.

Just for a moment, imagine that you are a three-year-old. Your parents love you but they really don't know how to handle you and in many ways you're in charge of the household. This is a scary realisation because, deep in your heart, you know that you're running the place. Your most scary thought is, 'If anything happens to me, who's going to help me?'

I love the statement of the character played by Tim Allen in *Home Improvement*. 'If I don't do anything in this parenting situation, I'm just one of the tall people who live in this house.' Children, especially boys, need leadership.

Lots of praise, and positive attention for doing the right thing

When you see your boy doing the right thing, or showing kindness or empathy, notice it and praise it. Talk about it later at dinner time. Tell, in front of Daddy, Grandma or the whole family, how proud you were and what a thoughtful boy he was that day. Choose him to have the honour of eating off the special family 'red' plate on Friday night. Put a spotlight on the great behaviour that your boy has shown, and help him progress toward your goal for him, of living happily and confidently in the world.

> ## HOT TIP ✔
>
> Bad behaviour with boys often comes because:
> - They're hungry.
> - They're tired.
> - They're frustrated.
>
> It's a wise adage that says 'when the river is low, the rocks show'. You need to feed them on time, make sure they get enough sleep and help them to handle frustration.

Monitoring the family rules
Be visual with small boys

Have three essential family rules:
- You mustn't hurt others.
- You mustn't hurt things.
- You mustn't hurt yourself.

To reinforce these rules:

- Put small coins, such as 10p pieces, in a jar.
- Pick one issue, like being kind or 'first-time obedience'.
- Every time your boy does something great, add money, and accompany it with lots of praise: 'That's great, Jakob', 'That is really thinking of someone else', 'We're so proud of you'.
- If he infringes one of the family rules, take a coin out. 'I'm sorry. I'm going to have to take out 10p.'

Keep the outcomes close to the actions so the boys 'get' it. Small boys do not have long attention spans so they need to see the pay-off quickly.

After two days of using the jar, take them to the pound shop and buy a present with the money they have accumulated. Show the rewards of doing the right thing.

Use compliments wisely

General, non-specific compliments like 'You're great' or 'You're a nice kid' might be pleasant and always welcome, but they are not as effective as focused, precise compliments for specific activities.

General compliments may raise the tone and sweeten the atmosphere, but specific compliments 'reinforce' behaviours, and make a child aware of exactly what it is that has pleased his parent.

'Thank you, Jamie, for putting the sandpit toys away. That will help them last a long time.'

'That's great that you helped your brother carry his bag — that was very caring of you.'

'Wow! Helping Mummy like that makes my job so much easier. You are a true helper!'

Your precise praise carries with it a clear description of what they did, why it is appreciated and, very often, a 'label' that children can use to describe themselves: a helper, a kind person, a good problem-solver.

Heroes-in-training sometimes make mistakes

A friend's small son, aged three and a half, rang 999 for no valid reason, even though his parents had carefully coached him in what an 'emergency' was. To the young culprit's dismay, and his mother's surprise, a police car arrived at their house and two uniformed officers knocked at the door. On being questioned over who made the call, the young adventurer vehemently denied any involvement. As his mother made eye contact with the young policeman, they both sensed the opportunity. Taking the cue, the policeman spoke kindly yet firmly to the small boy about the seriousness of the call. He explained that, by coming out to his house unnecessarily, some other very important calls could be missed. Someone could be knocked over on the road or a bad person not be caught. The child listened quietly, visibly shrinking before the imposing figure in front of him.

Later that evening, as his dad was sitting on the bed for their end-of-day chat, the burden of guilt overwhelmed the little boy and he confessed, with tears, that it was he who had rung 999. The father again reinforced the seriousness of the misadventure, while gently coaching his young son into a plan to put right what he had done.

First thing next morning, with dad holding his little boy's hand, they headed off to the local police station. There they had an interview with the officer concerned and the small boy, with his dad's support, apologised for what he had done.

With his conscience clear, dad and the boy visited the ice cream shop, before going home to relate what had happened. Young heroes who make mistakes can be helped to put it right, and to move on.

Children whose parents coach them into problem solving will grow up knowing that they can think for themselves, that no problem is too big to be solved and that mum and dad believe in them.

HOT TIP ✔

TEACH YOUR SON MANNERS – IT MAY PROTECT HIM FROM CRIME

Teaching your son manners is a powerful outward expression that acknowledges human dignity in everyone. Studies have shown that little children who are taught good manners do not get involved in crime. A well-known proverb says 'It's the little foxes that destroy the grapevines'.

Teaching good manners to your son fits into the broken-window theory: the idea that if small problems like loitering or not paying bus fares are eliminated, then large crimes will diminish, as has been shown in New York. In the same way, teaching manners prevents the windows from being broken in the first place, thus creating safer communities.

Creating a civil family, or society, begins with words like 'please' and 'thank you'.

Don't allow your shy boy to become a rude boy

Teach your son how to communicate and empower him with social skills. Don't let him hide behind his shyness.

If he has got into the habit of hiding away and refusing to look people in the eye and say 'Hello', you need to insist that he learns to — because it is something that you do in your family.

Allow your young son to practise on someone safe, such as a grandparent, but insist that he complies. Keep the greeting simple, but you need to win the battle if not speaking has become his way of getting attention or control. Say 'You need to say hello to Grandma and Granddad, and we're not going in until you say hello nicely.' Stay calm, but let him know that this is non-negotiable by taking him back to the car until he is ready. Take the paper with you to read so he knows that you are going nowhere until he does what he is asked.

Teach your boy how to hold a conversation. Use the tennis ball trick, where you say something, then throw a tennis ball to him. He has to reply and throw the tennis ball back to you. Carry on the conversation using the tennis ball to guide the flow. This helps your boy to visualise how conversations work.

Tell stories around the dinner table — family legends and stories about funny things they or their cousins have done.

IN SUMMARY 👁

WHAT PRESCHOOL BOYS NEED

Preschool boys need:

- A safe environment that meets their physical needs.
- A secure framework for their exploration and learning.
- Relaxed, confident parents who create appropriate boundaries.
- A calm atmosphere that promotes co-operation.
- To be busy and able to fulfil their insatiable need to learn.
- Lots of physical touch and closeness.
- Loving parents who are approachable, decisive, practical and clear.
- Routines and consistency.
- Lots of new experiences and outings.
- Fun with safe wider family and friends.

Chapter 7

The middle years – your window of opportunity

The most important human endeavour is the striving for morality in our actions. Our inner balance and even our very existence depends on it. Only morality in our actions can give beauty and dignity to our lives.

– Albert Einstein

Reading to your child is not only an opportunity to develop emotional closeness, but also an opportunity to develop his moral imagination.

– Jayne Sommers

None of the boys I see before me in the courts are involved in sport.

– Andrew Becroft, New Zealand Principal Youth Court Judge

The middle or pre-puberty years give you a special opportunity to form bonds of understanding and support that will carry your boy through into the next decade. Sadly, because boys of this age tend to be independent and straightforward, many parents just take life as it comes, without thinking deeply about the sort of young man they wish to launch into the world. Yet the period between six and ten years of age is your special opportunity to coach your son in all the capabilities that will enable him to grow into a resourceful, contributing adult.

Boys respond to leadership

The primary school years are your best years as parents. Boys at this age tend to want to know what is right and wrong. They like to know the rules, enjoy black and white boundaries and, especially, want to know what mum and dad think. So use these years positively and you are much more likely to have a great ride through the 'whitewater rafting' of the teenage years to come.

HOT TIP ✔

Boys like to know:
- Who is in charge?
- What are the rules?
- Will the rules be enforced in a fair way?

These are also years when your son is learning what it is to be a boy. He loves to be around men, and plays mostly with his male friends. The rough-and-tumble and boy games, the outdoor activities, forts in trees and sport will figure largely in these years. Boys who grow up on farms thrive in an environment where they can test themselves in the great outdoors and learn from men how to become competent at physical tasks. Unfortunately, in our risk-averse society, boys are being limited in what they are allowed to do. The activities that are replacing those once physical ones are mostly electronic, and they negatively affect boys in many ways.

I spoke at a rural school on parenting boys and was surprised that they were having a 'tractor day'. When I asked why boys growing up on farms would be so excited about a tractor day, I was told that, because of the mechanisation of farms and safety regulations, fathers no longer took their boys out with them on their daily rounds. So the grandfathers were bringing their tractors to school for the big experience.

A sense of mission and belonging

These are the years when you come into your own as a parent-coach, a manager and a leader for your son. There are special challenges in our modern world for boys growing up in an urban environment surrounded by electronics, cyber-space and online games that you, as a parent, will need to manage. You may need to take charge and determine how his hours are spent, in order to prevent his life being dominated by electronic media. In the absence of the open spaces we may have enjoyed as children, you may have to create these experiences for your boys.

Allow him the adventures of boyhood. Take him fishing, camping and exploring. Boys love to belong to a group, so make sure that your family is his favourite group to belong to during these years. As mentioned in Chapter 1, John Eldredge, author of *Wild at Heart*, suggests that deep in his heart every little boy longs for a battle to win and an adventure to live. The heart of a boy has its own dreams and is to be valued. The games in the backyard, and the adventures he thinks up, are all about pitting himself against the odds.

One of the best childhood memories our two boys recall is the time we hiked, with another family, into the Tararua Ranges near Wellington in New Zealand and camped overnight. We walked in on a beautiful balmy evening, pitched the tents, sizzled our sausages and told stories by torchlight as we settled into our sleeping bags. However, we were rudely awoken in the middle of the night by torrential rain, and by morning we were washed out.

The boys have never forgotten the six-mile trek out of that bush in the pouring rain, beginning with a ride through the flooded river in a LandRover. We made up stories of jungle adventures and 'eked' out our meagre rations. We were cold, wet and tired. But that memory for our boys is one of their best and the eventual hot bath has never been enjoyed as much. It was an adventure!

Michael Gurian, in *The Good Son*, suggests that one reason we see so much hyperactivity among boys in contemporary society is an overloading of media exposure.

'We have nearly 3,000,000 boys on Ritalin (in the US), the primary medical treatment for attention-span problems with ADD and ADHD. Many of these boys are just little Huck Finns, normal boys whose emotions the culture wants to suppress with medicine — but many do actually have attention span problems. Why so many attention problems in the last few decades among our males?

'Specialists think what is happening is this: our media intake, activities orientation, lack of reflection and prayer time, and chaotic physical environments (e.g. busy city environments, where ADD and ADHD are more common) are over-stimulating the male brain in ways it's not set up to handle. It is becoming normal for young boys to be over-stimulated. A hundred years ago, boys had more reflection time and, of course, no visual media intake. Now, our boys' lives are less supervised and more hyper-stimulated. Neurologists often call our present child environment "hyper-mediated" because it includes so much media input and other distractions.

'If you are noticing problems with your son's attention span abilities, diagnosis is important, as well as a concerted effort to de-stimulate his day. Turn off the radios, music, TV, video games, computers. The over-stimulation is locking his brain down, or "freezing" it.'

The opportunity to try out and master skills

Between the ages of six and twelve years, encourage your boy to develop a number of skills. It is especially valuable if he is encouraged to become particularly proficient in at least one area. Experiment with skills, hobbies and sport and support him as he builds these interests. Self-esteem is not built on what other people say, but on what the child himself knows about his own abilities.

Allow him to become an expert in something. If he is not a gifted sportsman, still ensure that he remains in a team sport, but allow him to pursue a hobby or interest that may be more his thing. Stamp collecting, go-carting, photography and music are just some examples. Encourage him to become competent so that in some area he feels himself to be an expert, or at least ahead of his peers. When life is giving him a hard time, it means he won't hit rock bottom about his own value and worth.

He'll be able to say to himself, 'No, I'm good at this, I'm able to hold my own in this area of endeavour.' It's sort of a trampoline of self-esteem that causes him to bounce back: 'I may have bombed out here, but I'm a good batsman at cricket.' Or, 'I know how to bait a line to catch a good trout.'

Being around men teaches him how to do 'man-things'

Dads especially can capitalise on this window of time to build comradeship with their sons. Share a hobby or a sport together, something that your son genuinely enjoys such as cricket, fishing, a tradition of going to a sports event or concert together, golf, tennis, boating or even video games. When your son becomes a teenager he may pull away and look outside the family or more to his friends, but if you are already allies and have a history of playing a game, building stuff or hiking together, there will be some common ground for you to draw on.

The proverbial stage when your son, at about the age of fourteen, is amazed how dumb his dad is, still tends to occur. However, at the age of , he'll be amazed how much his dad has learnt in five years. So keep the connection and be patient. (It is interesting to note that this phase was noted by Mark Twain — little has changed in a century or so!)

So, if you've been good mates between the ages of six and twelve, then through those early adolescent years, when he is gently pushing you away and taking control of his own life (maybe even hero-worshipping other men), you will still have a tangible link with his life.

School and your boy

Boys learn teachers rather than subjects, so your boy's teacher is important. A teacher can block a boy from learning if they clash. Where a girl can get around the teacher to get to the subject, a boy will tend to switch off.

Parents can help a boy to get on with his teacher by teaching him to SLANT:

- **S**it up
- **L**ook interested
- **A**cknowledge
- **N**od occasionally
- **T**rack the teacher with your eyes

This will also heal a relationship between your son and his teacher, if it's broken down.

— Professor Ian Lillico, Gender Institute, Griffith University

It is great when his teacher is a good storyteller, has a sense of humour, believes in rules, is fair and is passionate about the subject. A good teacher acts like a good parent, and a good parent like a good teacher. Boys will respond to the atmosphere in the classroom.

Boys convert feelings into movement, and a good teacher will understand this. So it is better to have disruptive boys run around the sportsfield three times than have them sit still to think about what they're doing.

Boys learn when they are given projects, and have to report what they have learnt back to the class. It appeals to the male sense of finding solutions and gives them a sense of mastery. If a boy has to teach you something, he will learn as well.

Boys learn photographically. Get them to 'read' photos — get them to look at photos and quiz them on the details, the meaning of the story. Get them to describe pictures. It greatly improves their literacy and their ability to interpret situations, which in turn improves other subjects.

If your son is struggling at school or switching off, you may want to tune him into an interest that really engages his imagination.

> What children hear, they mostly forget.
>
> What they see, they mostly remember.
>
> What they do, they understand and internalise.

Build your family into a team —
the power of 'we'

They don't care that you know, until they know that you care.

Many parents find it helpful during these years to set up a family mission statement. It's sort of like saying together, 'This is who we are and what we stand for'. Boys especially love the sense of team, and usually 'buy in' to the family values readily when they have been part of an exercise such as this. Many families say that rivalry, meanness and so on fade away after they have involved the children in writing a mission statement for their family. Blended families find it a great way for everyone to understand what the family stands for, and what expectations everyone has of each other.

It is especially the supportive statements that children tend to like, such as, 'We will always stick up for each other and be loyal to each other.' One family we know have as their family motto, 'You can count on Me!'

In his book *The Power of the Family*, Paul Pearsall suggests that the family is the key to a child sensing that he is capable and able to think for himself. In fact, he says, it is the healthy family rituals that create a sense of belonging and significance that are the real key. He suggests that boys who don't take part in healthy family rituals will often go looking for them in the violence offered in gangs. In healthy families, the children join a family that already stands for something. It is the sense that 'in our family we always do this, or we always expect this' that gives children that sense of rightness and inner strength.

Parents have a responsibility to lead in their family. All children need leadership, and if parents don't lead them, they will look for someone else who displays leadership, negatively or positively.

I have often noticed that some of the best parents I have talked to, who tend to have boys with good self-esteem and confidence, talk about their families in terms of 'we'. For instance, the family rules began with 'we' rather than 'you'.

For example, 'We all pitch in to keep this house tidy and liveable' rather than 'You have to keep your rooms tidy'. Rather than saying, 'You must call if you are late' it was statements like 'We always check with home if we are going to be late'. That gives a shared sense of ownership and responsibility. In other words, we parents 'own' the rules, and live by them as well. The power of using 'we' instead of 'you' gives you a chance to encourage your boys to take responsibility, to manage their own affairs and to consider the needs and rights of others. These little day-by-day practices gradually seep into your children's habits and become the blueprint for the way they are likely to live.

It is unlikely that you will always stick to all your family rules, but they will give you the 'railway lines' as it were for your family to run on, and be a basis for negotiation when they head into those teenage years.

HOT TIP ✔

Some ideas for your family rules:

- We use manners: 'Excuse me', 'Please', 'Thank you', 'I'm sorry'.
- We don't insult people or behave rudely.
- We don't ridicule anyone who tries.
- We don't use vulgar language.
- We don't interrupt; we wait our turn to speak.
- We presume people are innocent. We first listen to their side of the story before we jump to conclusions.
- We do not make promises that we don't expect to carry out.
- We respect each other's property and right to privacy.
- We show respect for older people.
- We respect others' cultures and beliefs.
- We celebrate each other's accomplishments.

- We practise good telephone manners.
- We don't bring outdoor activities indoors: no ball throwing, running and chasing, missile throwing, rough wrestling or excessive shouting.
- If we argue over TV or games, we get one warning to stop; if quarrelling persists, the activity is terminated.

Obviously you will not want to overload your children with zillions of rules, but introducing them and incorporating them into the family, a few at a time, makes life so much easier. Have a family minute book and write down your family decisions over the years.

Cleanliness and order may be a high priority for you, but they are likely to be low priority for your boy. Negotiate realistically on those issues.

ACTION LAB

MINISTER OF JUSTICE

If you have more than one child, rotate the privilege of being 'Minister of Justice'. When it is their turn, they have certain privileges and authority.

They get to decide where they sit in the car, what channel to watch, and to arbitrate if there is an argument over who has the first shower. (Of course, their authority is still subject to yours.)

JOB ALLOCATION

Put the shared family jobs in a hat, and get everyone to choose one. Decide if you will all work together with favourite music playing or if each person will do them at their convenience. Give them the challenge of setting a new 'world record' for a task or set a time-limit for completion.

The family meal table

Your boys live in a world which, in many ways, is rough on them. The media presents half-truths and negative events, and the world of boys is often staunch and cruel. Your family needs to be a safe place to which your boys can retreat.

The family dinner table should provide a forum where your kids can unload, share jokes, be dusted down and picked up, given some adult perspective and wisdom and sent out to face their world again strengthened and supported. Around the dinner table your boys can debate ideas, learn how to use their brain as a sieve not just a sponge, enjoy sharing their life and discuss with you, the adults, the big questions of life.

Because society shows little consensus about personal boundaries and modes of behaviour, you need to 'turn up the volume' on your family values. In the context of fun, two-way communication and lots of celebration of each individual, your boys can absorb and practise those ideals of character that you value.

At the dinner table:

- Read, followed by questions and quizzes.
- Inspire your son with books, especially stories of men who are honourable and decent.
- Ask your boys what they think.
- Ask your boys how they feel.
- Ask them 'What if' questions. For example, what would they do if they found themselves in a group that was bullying other kids?
- Get your boys to rate their day out of ten. Ask them why they give a particular day that rating.

HOT TIP ✔

QUESTIONS THAT CAN'T BE ANSWERED 'YES' OR 'NO' – PRACTISING CONVERSATION WITH YOUR SON

Children trust people who are tuned into their needs. Taking time to ask considered questions and listen to the answers is a powerful expression of love. It's risky to presume you know what your boy's thinking about.

Good eye-contact can make the difference between success and failure in many situations. Practising this skill through family discussions and interactions will help good conversation become natural for your son.

Questions to jump-start conversations

- Describe the person you would like to be in ten years.
- What are your three favourite songs, movies, books, TV shows?
- What do you enjoy most about them?
- How much do you think it costs to run and fund our family?
- When you think about your future, what are you most excited about or afraid of?
- What does it mean to be a leader?
- Who are the three greatest people you've ever learned about?
- Why do bad things happen to good people and good things happen to bad people sometimes?
- What is your favourite time of day?
- Is there someone in your life you don't like to be around? What bothers you the most about him or her?
- If you were Mum or Dad, what would your top five rules be?
- What do you like more — being alone or being with other people? Why?

Passing on ethical beliefs and behaviours

Honesty, courage, friendship, persistence, faith — all these are traits of good character. But in order for our boys to recognise and develop these qualities, we must give them examples of right and wrong, good and bad. Between six and ten years of age is a wonderful time to share the wealth of literature and stories from history of people who acted with these qualities. Mix old and new stories such as the Aesop fables, *Tom Sawyer, Beauty and the Beast* and stories from your faith tradition, along with the Narnia tales and stories of modern heroes who achieved great things with their lives. This wealth of stories and ideas, together with your coaching, will to some extent program their moral hard-drive, giving them a 'plumbline' to measure their actions against.

Get into the habit of reading as a family — on cold nights in front of the fire, on holiday or around the dinner table. Read a chapter at a time and enjoy the family closeness — it will give you all a break from the electronic media. The stories you read as a family will also be a springboard for discussions about their own lives. In the same way, choose videos and DVDs carefully and watch them together.

Stories passed down from parents to children are also a powerful method for handing on the values of community and faith. In Jewish culture, for instance, there's an ancient custom for families to retell the story of the Exodus from Egypt every year at the Passover meal table. Whether you are a religious family or not, all children can benefit from knowing moral codes, such as the Ten Commandments, just as children are taught nursery rhymes and classic tales as part of their literary heritage. Stories of heroes in their own family's past can also be a great way of instilling pride and values into your sons.

Complicating the job of parenting today is confusion about whether there is even such a thing as ethical absolutes. As our society has become more individualistic and materialistic, it can be a real challenge to identify what your family stands for. We heard recently of a parental debate over a local primary school motto which had traditionally been 'Come in and Learn; Go out and Serve'. Some parents felt it should be changed to 'Come in and Learn, Go out and Succeed'.

While this may be understandable in the context of parents' educational goals, we sell our children short and condemn them to only half a life if their world view is based only on individualistic values. Ethics, by their nature, are based on how we treat others.

What have we learnt from the past several thousand years of civilisation about basic decency? That it is wrong to steal, to lie, to break promises, to mistreat a child, to humiliate someone, to torment an animal, or to think only of yourself. On the positive side, it is right to be considerate, respectful of others, charitable and generous. Think about your favourite and most successful friends and acquaintances, and ask anyone who comes from a loving family. Wonderful, loving relationships tend to grow with unselfishness and sacrifice. Children are not born altruistic; it's our privilege as parents to nurture them from being self-centred to becoming outwardly focused, loving and principled human beings. It's important we do what civilised cultures have always done, and pass along our moral traditions to the next generation.

Many of today's children often hear a clear message of how special they are and have been taught to stand up for themselves and fight for their rights. As parents we need to balance this message with other values, such as the importance of behaving truthfully, thinking of others and practising generosity.

The fact is, children need values to negotiate the inevitable moral dilemmas of life. They also need big people who will show them how to live well and who will hold the line for them as they develop their own internal disciplines.

HOT TIP ✔

ANGER!

Anger from our children often brings out the anger in us. Our response to them models to them what to do with anger.

What can you do with anger? You can repress it into passive aggression, blow up, or reprocess it into either useful action or a more appropriate emotion. Give your child the gift of processing anger so they know they have options.

- When they feel angry, they can go somewhere to cool off.
- Let your child know you are available to talk about their feelings.
- Forcing a boy to talk while he is still flooded with hot emotions might escalate, rather than calm and clarify the situation.
- Give him a plan.
- Go over the steps of what to do next time he feels so mad.

Gaining confidence

Does your boy know that he is trusted to do certain tasks? Is that part of his belonging to your family? Growing up with a strong sense of community helps children to have a greater sense of meaning, purpose and belonging. As well, when a boy helps deliver a cake to a friend in distress, or uses initiative to help out when a neighbour's house floods, he learns that initiative, creativity and the ability to act autonomously when needed are all possible and valuable.

Allow your boys to express pain or sadness

Make your home a safe place emotionally. Developmental psychologist Mary Polce-Lynch, author of *Boy Talk: How You Can Help Your Son Express His Emotions*, says that, as a psychotherapist, she has worked with too many boys who tell her their parents are great about attending their sports games, but never ask them what's going on inside of them. So the boys never tell. 'Too often, it seems, boys grow up in a situation where there is no acceptable way for them to talk with others about their inner feelings, except for perhaps when they are teenagers and they talk with their girlfriends. But this is way too late,' Polce-Lynch says.

Boys may not naturally constantly express their feelings as girls do but, if they need to, home should be the place where they can share, without fear of rejection or ridicule. Discuss issues that have arisen at school, and talk about what your son's friends feel or think. It will help your boy work out what he thinks. Talk about what he did or plans to do about a particular situation that is worrying him. Take him for a walk or an outing. Shoulder to shoulder is a comfortable way for your boy to talk.

HOT TIP ✔

LISTEN TO YOUR SONS – IT IS THE SAME AS LOVING THEM

- As your boys grow, try to monitor your parental tendency to ask too many questions, lecture and give advice.

- There are times to share advice and it will be better received if we learn to nod and say as little as possible. For example, if your son is telling you he was told off at school, say, 'It sounds like you were embarrassed.'
- Get your son to tell you more. Use nods and mmmms and leave it at that.
- If your boy tells you he left his togs at home so he couldn't go swimming, check yourself before you jump in with, 'Well, that's because you were late up and didn't get yourself organised.' *He'll already know that.* Instead, try 'It sounds like you really wanted to swim with the others' and leave it at that!

Showing love through traditions

Traditions are like beacons in family life. They are events our boys can count on, that let them know not only that they are part of a family, but also an individual who matters. We can make certain each of our boys receives positive, focused attention by creating family traditions that we build into our daily lives. Warm family traditions will ensure that the family is the strongest and most persuasive influence in your son's life.

A good friend told me how it had been the tradition in their family to make a banner for each person on their birthday. The banner was always a surprise, which was there in the morning for the child to wake up to, and it was always themed around whatever the family member was 'into' at the time. Her 16-year-old son, realising that she was tired and under pressure on the eve of his sister's birthday, suggested 'Mum, would you like me to make the banner for Sarah?' My friend observed that it would probably not have been a particularly 'cool' thing for a sixteen-year-old boy to suggest, but because it had always been a tradition, he took it for granted that someone would do it!

Four great things about boys

Boys are very loyal. Boys may get into fights if friends or family are mocked. For example, if someone says something nasty about his sister.

Boys have healthy egos. They are usually very resilient and will get over things quickly.

Boys have amazing raw intelligence. They love quizzes.

Boys are very competitive. This can help in getting jobs done to a high standard. They prefer exams to ongoing assignments.

The optimistic boy

During these middle years we can inoculate our boys against depression and cynicism by giving them a sense of mastery over their own lives, a sense that they can take action that will make a difference. 'Learned helplessness' comes from believing 'I can't do anything about what is happening to me'. That attitude leads to passivity and pessimism. Pessimism hardens like a shell on a child's life and colours their whole attitude towards life.

Therefore, 'age-appropriate' choices and 'deals' with boys are essential. They build a sense that consequences are largely the result of their own choices and are therefore their responsibility. This gives a boy a sense of power over his own life that will enable him to accept the unchangeable, but work to improve his circumstances where possible.

A Wellington coroner recently made the comment after a spate of youth suicides that, in New Zealand, we have created a society where our boys are protected from failure. He observed that we must allow our boys to fail sometimes, so they know how to get back into life, back off the bench, and back to the drawing board if they have received a knock-back.

HOT TIP ✔

Resilience is built through giving our sons healthy messages,
communicated from a supportive and encouraging parent,
such as:

- 'It's OK to do a job badly, while you are learning.'
- 'Mistakes are OK. Mistakes can be fixed.'
- 'There are always other choices we can make.'

Persistence, organisation, confidence and striving towards goals — these
are the qualities we must help our sons develop and we must reassure
them that we believe they have the character to come through.

Barbara Coloroso believes that our children develop inner strength
when we give them the following messages through the way we interact
with them. I cannot put them better than she does in *Kids Are Worth It*,
and so have asked for permission to use them in my seminars. Verbally
and non-verbally our boys need to hear from us:

- I believe in you.
- I know you can handle this.
- I trust you.
- You are cared for.
- You are listened to.
- You are very important to me.

Goals create energy, and they give boys a future

Self-esteem is rooted in a sense of progress. Help your son to set achievable
goals, then celebrate when he achieves them. Whether it is to get into the
soccer team, or to save for a bicycle, working towards the goal and the
celebration and sense of achievement when he reaches it are building his
EQ (emotional intelligence) and his skills.

HOT TIP ✔

Sport is vital for boys because it is a great teacher about life. Sport will teach your son how to:

- Play within the rules.
- Listen to the coach.
- Be a good winner.
- Lose graciously.
- Develop his own skills.
- Be a team player.

Boys who don't enjoy sport

I believe we should encourage an interest in a sport of some sort in all boys (and girls). Understanding the rules of tennis, rugby, netball, cricket and so on are actually social skills for a boy, and he will always be able to join in groups of men and boys if he can converse at some level about sport.

But there are many options other than the 'traditional' sports. We are fortunate in New Zealand to have sports such as sailing, horse riding, tennis, golf and archery, as well as the many other team sports and cultural groups accessible to most. Cubs and Scouts, Boys Brigade and schools offer opportunities to try many different sports in a safe environment. For boys who aren't physical, table tennis or billiards, chess or self-defence disciplines such as karate or tae kwon do are other options.

It is OK to insist, especially for your school-age son, that he completes the year/term at a chosen sport or activity. Boys often have to taste a little success before they will risk making an all-out effort. So tow them out on the 'biscuit' before trying them on skis, move closer to the target for the first couple of shots, give yourself a ridiculous handicap in the first round — whatever it takes to make their initial experience a success. Of course, losing teaches him wonderful lessons in life too, but put it further down in the curriculum. Sometimes you need to get them to try a couple of times before they will realise that they enjoy it.

By emphasising sport, I don't suggest that you neglect teaching your son to cook, babysit, do first aid and all the other things that round out a family and a life. The best way to teach these things is by allowing them to become capable at one thing at a time. If it's cooking, perfect one recipe and encourage him to make it regularly each week, such as 'Ben's carrot salad' or 'Isaac's apple crumble'. A simple ritual, such as dad making pancakes for the family on Sunday mornings with the boys, will give them the idea of success and appreciation in the kitchen. If there is no dad, it can be your boy's own task, with a little coaching initially, followed by lots of praise and affirmation, preferably in front of the grandparents!

Progressive, age-appropriate choices

Every boy likes to sense that he is progressing; that as he matures he is being given more and more opportunities to make some choices. Allow even your small boys to make age-appropriate choices, and to live with the outcomes. They will learn to make good choices as they practise on the little decisions.

Give a child choice when it doesn't really matter, for example, that awful orange and purple combination of clothes that your seven-year-old loves will not affect the survival of the species!

If you tend to be a 'dominant' parent, learn to say 'yes' whenever possible. Learn to use phrases like: 'Yes, when . . . ', 'Yes, if . . .', 'Yes, after . . .'

Help him get organised

Most boys need help in getting organised. A whiteboard by his bed and firm routines for morning and night will help.

When things go wrong, ask him to come up with a plan to make sure they go right next time. The pain of getting wet and cold because he forgot his raincoat, or the hunger caused by leaving his lunch behind, will be a great teacher.

HOT TIP ✔

PORTABLE JOB CARDS

If you want your son to be ready for school on time, then break his tasks into bite-size pieces. Write them on a card which he can carry with him. The 'morning' card could look something like this:

Morning routine

- Rise and shine — 7.15am.
- Make bed.
- Get dressed.
- Have breakfast.
- Empty dishwasher.
- Clean teeth.
- Check everything is in school bag.
- Kiss mum goodbye!

If your child is easily distracted, simply ask 'Where are you up to on your job card?'

Give a reward on Friday night for a whole week of staying on-task.

Discipline — firm, fair and friendly

What doesn't work with boys:

- Stand-over techniques.
- Blaming.
- Threats and commands.
- Lectures and moralising.
- Warnings.
- Martyrdom statements.
- Sarcasm.
- Prophesy ('You'll have no friends').

They go off into another world.

What works better:
- Describe what you see.
- Give information ('Milk turns sour').
- Say it with a word ('Fridge').
- Write a note.

— Ian Lillicoe

Let your boy own his own problems

Many parents rescue their sons, but then get frustrated and angry at them. Keep your boy's problem firmly in his own court, but take anger out of the equation. Your anger will actually be counter-productive and stop him taking responsibility, because he will be dealing with your emotion, not thinking about the problem.

Offer all the support he needs to solve his problem. Separate the behaviour and your son as a person. Label him positively: 'You're a good kid . . . this isn't like you' or something similar, and empathise with your boy about the problem. Stay on his side.

Problem + consequences − parental anger = lesson learned

Avoid putting your son on the defensive

When your boy makes a bad decision, he doesn't need a lecture — he just needs a good plan to fix it. 'So let's go through that story again . . . the seagull flew in the window, left his cricket ball right there and then flew out again . . . is that the story?'

Give him time to tell the truth and then identify the problem, so that you can work on a solution.

When he leaves his gym gear behind, don't rush to the school with it. Give him one free delivery, but explain that from now on he is on his own. He will no longer have you to rescue him. But he will have your empathy and support. Say something like, 'That's a problem, son. You'll need to work out a good plan to make sure it doesn't happen next time.'

Boys tend to be great problem-solvers, if given the chance.

Boys like clear instructions and simple rules. Rules without reasons tend to lead to rebellion, so don't surprise your kids with new family rules. Work them out together.

HOT TIP ✔

- **Establish family rules** and use phrases such as, 'Remember the rules. In our family we talk politely to each other' or 'We're not a hitting family'.
- When asking a boy to do something, **give the instruction with a time limit**. Smile, and keep a lift in your voice, communicating that you are expecting compliance. 'I'd like you to clean your room by lunchtime.' 'You can go out to play after you have fed the cat.'
- **Let the consequences do the teaching**.
- **Have clear rules and administer them fairly** – without anger.
- **Allow natural justice to occur** – the bike is left out so it gets put away until the weekend.
- **Have appropriate consequences** (these may be a combination of putting things right, having time out, withdrawal of privileges or something he cares about (TV, computer, PlayStation time).
- **Acknowledge that different treatment for different children of different ages is appropriate** (bedtimes, for example). Fair doesn't necessarily mean equal.
- **Follow through**, and remember that the certainty of consequences is more important than their severity.

> ## Restore the relationship after your boy has been in trouble
>
> CPR is a life-saving term. When you are dealing with a discipline issue with your son, you can use this term as a checklist:
>
> **Consequence** – a penalty that will teach.
>
> **Plan** – to put right what he has done and how he will avoid it in the future.
>
> **Reconciliation** – relationships restored.

Several years ago a friend of mine, a busy working mother, answered a phone call at work from her nine-year-old son. He said he was at their local corner shop where he'd been caught stealing a chocolate bar. The proprietor had given the young boy the choice of ringing his mother or the police. His mother immediately took a taxi to the shop.

She talked with her son and he acknowledged how wrong the action had been, and apologised to the shop owner. His mother then worked out with him a way he could make restitution. The young boy agreed to sweep out the shop there and then, plus spend an hour each day for the next week doing errands for the owner. By taking decisive action this mother turned a regrettable incident into a valuable life-lesson.

Establishing a strong deterrent against ever trying shoplifting again helped the boy understand the more fundamental lesson of why stealing in all forms is wrong. Today he's a well-adjusted and law-abiding young man. Amazingly, the shop owner told my friend that, of all the times he'd caught young shoplifters, this was the first time a parent had ever responded when called.

Types of parents

I'd like to warn you of the possible outcomes of missing the importance of these middle years. They are preparation for the teenage years to come, when your boy will be establishing his identity, struggling to be seen as his own person, and finding his place in the world.

During parenting seminars I talk about different parenting styles (described below by John Cowan). You may recognise them!

Parentus-sergeant majorcus

You usually can't recognise this species by the way they look, but you can pick them by the types of noises they make, noises such as, 'I don't have to give you a reason. Just do it, because I'm your parent and I say so!'

Recognise the style? Lots of rules and instructions, but very few reasons; harsh discipline, but not much emotional support. Too many parents behave like this. Perhaps it's the only style of parenting they saw when they were growing up, or perhaps they have chosen this kind of parenting because 'I want my kids to turn out perfectly. I'm going to put so many rules and regulations around them that they won't have a chance to put a foot wrong.'

How do kids of this kind of parent respond — especially when they hit adolescence? They rebel. They might be very well-behaved little boys (they had no option), but as teenagers, they kick over the traces.

Why? Because the rules were not presented with reasons; the children never believed that the things they were prohibited from doing by their parents were actually wrong. Instead, they just thought their parents were killjoys. And, because they knew that breaking the rules would be severely punished, the children became very good at not being caught. They learned how to look good but still do stuff behind their parents' back.

But the real tragedy for boys of *parentus-sergeant majorcus* is: you can understand their not liking their parents, but they tend to not even like themselves. They often have crushingly low self-esteem, probably because they didn't get any of that praise and affirmation that little boys need as they grow up. Or perhaps they only ever heard the 'Try harder' message from their parents.

Parentus-jellyfishicus

We also identify the *parentus-jellyfishicus* and the *parentus-absentus* as sub-groups of parental species, both of whom leave children with unresolved security and self-control issues.

Parentus-jellyfishicus says things like, 'Are you in trouble at school again? Those awful teachers, they gang up on you, don't they? Why don't you have a day off school so you feel better; we'll have your favourite food for tea.' Or, 'So you want to watch that movie on television tonight. It's on awfully late, and I'd hate you to be too tired at school, but I'll do your paper run so you can sleep in.'

Maybe there aren't many parents quite as wet as this, but *parentus-jellyfishicus* parents are far from uncommon. Their main characteristic is that they fail to set limits and boundaries for their boys. You often see this type of parent in the supermarket, with their small boy thrashing around on the floor while the parent says, 'Isn't he a little character; I can't do a thing with him.' This becomes a self-fulfilling prophecy!

Imagine that your eight-year-old child is allowed to use your tools to build a boat. You come home and find your best hammer lying on the ground, going rusty.

The *parentus-sergeant majorcus* will rush inside and yell, 'You stupid little twit! That's the last time you are ever going to use my tools. You know the rules. That's it, get out of here!'

Parentus-jellyfishicus will come in and say, 'Don't worry dear, I'll buy another hammer. It's good that you are being so creative.'

But the really thoughtful parent, who is working for his child's future — *parentus-backbonicus*? He is likely to come in and say, 'Look what I found on the drive. You've got a problem. But here's some steel wool — this hammer will need some elbow grease and some oil. Off you go now and have a go at cleaning it up. If you need a hand, come and get me.'

That parent knows that he can clean up the hammer in a fraction of the time. He knows that he will probably have to do it again anyway, but he sees it as a chance for his boy to learn how to own problems and solve them.

What is going to happen in fifteen years' time, when the boys of these different parenting styles have adult-sized problems? The child of *parentus-sergeant majorcus* will lock up with paralysis. Inside, this boy will still hear the yelling, even if no one is yelling in the real world. He will feel bad and will reach for anything that will take away the pain — a bottle, a pill or whatever.

The child of *parentus-jellyfishicus* will just walk away from it. 'Oh dear, what a mess. Someone else will sort it out.' Work hassle or relationship problem; it won't matter. This person will just run away.

But the boy of a *parentus-backbonicus* parent will say, 'Mmmm . . . I've got a problem. It is my problem, but I can solve it. There are no problems so big that they can't be solved.'

HOT TIP ✔

DOES YOUR BOY KNOW HOW TO OFFER A GENUINE COMPLIMENT?

'Not likely!' you may be thinking. But here is a great family tradition that can change the put-down culture of a home.

On every birthday, for both children and adults, have a family meal where everyone at the table makes a 'speech' about the birthday boy or girl. It might only be a brief sentence, but it needs to contain a genuine compliment and mention something about them that is appreciated. No put-downs, no insults, no damning with faint praise.

Start with birthdays and then practise this tradition as often as you can.

Use inspiration, not just behaviour modification

Don't underestimate your power to influence a future leader, or a man who will make sacrifices and pour energy into a great cause.

In her book *How Could You Do That?*, internationally syndicated New York radio superhost Laura Schlessinger tells how she began her radio career by trying to help people understand why they acted the way they did. Schlessinger has a PhD in biology and psychology, but it wasn't until she started interacting with people on her radio show that she had some fascinating revelations about how we tick.

The longer she spoke to members of the public about their lives, the more she came to believe that being human is about much more than just seeking survival and gratification. Schlessinger observed a human capacity for 'tenacity of spirit and nobility of purpose' that isn't necessarily explained simply by a person's biology or background.

She became increasingly convinced that *morality* gives human beings their special dignity, and causes people to transcend instinct. 'More and more I began to see that the problems people wanted to solve, resolve or avoid in the first place needed to be approached along the lines of right and wrong,' she says.

In response to this realisation, Schlessinger started talking about honour, integrity and ethics in tandem with the usual psychological concepts. BANG! Her radio programme took off and became an international phenomenon.

Sexuality in the 'in-between' years

In an ideal world, a boy's sexuality would normally be latent during these middle years. He is not particularly interested in girls, because his developmental task at this stage is to identify with what it is to be a man. Inevitably, puberty will arrive, his testosterone levels will soar and his head will be in a different place. He will become more oppositional and he will begin to look at the opposite sex in a different way.

However, these days, things are not that simple for this age group. We live in a sexualised culture. Your boys — even your young boys — are likely to be exposed to sexual images and even pornography. And the sad truth is that a boy's first sexual experience has a powerful imprinting effect. If a boy's sexuality is aroused inappropriately during these years, it will distort his views of sexuality and hinder his opportunity for true intimacy later in life. We do need to be vigilant in protecting our sons from inappropriate sexual images and predators; from paedophiles and other adults who lead them into situations that they do not have the maturity to handle.

Set boundaries on what sort of entertainment you allow your young son to be exposed to and explain to him how important it is that, in your family, you practise the 'swimming costume' rule. That is, that no one must touch you anywhere that your costume covers (except the doctor, if mum or dad is there). Be firm, and tell your small son that it is because this area is private and special, and only for a future day, with someone special. You don't want it to be a shameful or guilty subject, but you want to link it with a future dream. Answer his questions briefly without going into detail. He is usually just wanting the first layer of information at this age.

Keep in mind your future dream for your son

Every parent would like to see their son grow into a man who eventually experiences a loving, faithful relationship that offers true intimacy; a relationship that will allow him to enjoy a loving partnership of healthy interdependence. You need to prepare him for that ideal. Equip him with good information to make sure that he experiences positive, healthy imprinting and a great respect for his own body, as well as the bodies of others.

Appropriate attitudes

There is good reason for training young people in modesty — it is to do with personal boundaries and respect for oneself and others. Though it sounds vaguely prudish to put it down on paper, boys need to learn that, even though they have very handsome bodies, their natural tendency to get dressed in private is appropriate, and that other people need their privacy too.

Again, your own attitude to bodies and relationships will be the crucial thing. If you give them the idea that sex and bodies are a 'dirty' topic, if you over-react with anger or 'fluster' at their natural questions, it will instil a sense of taboo around these topics. Their curiosity will be unabated; in fact it will probably be heightened, but it is likely to be coupled with shame and guilt. They will look elsewhere for sexual information, which is all too available in sleazy magazines and inappropriate or ill-informed conversation.

> ## HOT TIP ✔
>
> If you find your son has been involved in inappropriate sexual activity, stay calm. Try not to over-react, but gather information about the incident and follow up. Always talk to your son in terms of future dreams when speaking about sexuality. For example, talk about the idea that one day he will meet someone special, and kissing and sex is especially for that person. This will put sex in the future context of love and security for your young son.

Your personal morality and beliefs about faithfulness, kindness, communication and self-control in relationships are likely to be taken on board by your son if he sees them modelled and explained in the home. If you communicate the high value of relationships and marriage to your children, they will expect to be valued and will value their future partners. Even if your circumstances are less than ideal, and not what you would choose for your son, you can still plant a dream for him that will influence the choices he makes about future relationships.

The best approach to these topics is one of casual good humour. Your sons should be aware that your bedroom door is locked at times, and what goes on in there is private, but that it is special and enjoyable.

Progressive teaching

When he is eight or nine years old, you will probably need to give your son a significant talk about sex. This is normally called 'The Talk'. However, this term tends to give the impression that a parent's responsibility towards a child's sex education is limited to one intense talk! This is not the case — it is natural and appropriate to drip-feed age-appropriate information to children throughout their childhood. Look for opportunities to talk, such as when there is a pregnancy in the family. It is OK to talk about right and wrong behaviour in the context of sex and relationships.

Before he heads off to school, a boy needs to know where babies come from (in general terms), some basic anatomy about boy–girl differences, and the appropriate names for parts of his body. Cute slang for body parts is okay, as long as he also learns that these parts have proper names as well. He also needs some information to keep him safe from abuse: what is appropriate touching, which adults he can go places with, and what to do if anything untoward does happen. Give him a password and teach him to never go with anyone who doesn't know the family password.

During these years, model warm expressions of love between you and your spouse. Let him see that you genuinely enjoy each other's company, and love each other on many different levels.

The 'big weekend' with Dad: forewarned is fore-armed

Before adolescence kicks in properly, plan a weekend away with your son. Make it a special event that your boy will look forward to for several years, and enjoy planning it with him.

It's not an opportunity to take him away for a private 'Where do babies come from?' talk — today's kids need that information much sooner than eleven. It's about sharing the information he needs now he is growing up.

It's a time to do 'boys things' together; maybe camping, fishing or some great thrill-rides at a touristy-type place. It's also a time to talk about things. But most of all it is likely to set the stage for a great time during adolescence.

Our organisation, Parents Inc., has produced a CD called *The Big Weekend*, which is designed for you to listen to with your son in the car (or even the tent) and to talk about the issues it raises, such as peer pressure, body changes, that terrible sense of inferiority that many teenagers feel, emotions, love, friendships and dating, and how values and faith affect these.

Because this weekend is a planned event, each of your boys is reassured that he will have the information he needs when the time comes. My colleague John Cowan, whose seven-year-old son had observed the tradition of his older brother going on a great weekend with dad, told me that this younger son had recently asked a question about sex at the dinner table. But before John could answer, the eight-year-old sister chimed in with, 'You're just going to have to wait until your trip when you are eleven!' John said with a smile, 'Knowledge is great, but so are mystery, and anticipation and the thrill of knowing that you are going to know.'

A good friend, Scott, who is also the father of three, took each of his two boys away for a 'Big Weekend' when they turned twelve. This tradition began with their daughter and became a given as the boys also reached that milestone. He says, 'The pay-off for the investment of that weekend has been huge in the choices the children have made over the years, in my relationship with each child, and in their developing characters through adolescence and beyond.'

After hearing what Scott and his sons have done, it was easy to see how all boys would be thrilled to connect with their dad in this way, enjoying his undivided attention and company for a special weekend.

Their weekends had been talked about for several years, and were something that both boys had looked forward to. Because of their different personalities, and because the boys themselves were part of the planning process, the weekends took different forms with each son. The only non-negotiable part was that dad and son would listen to a set of tapes and would discuss stuff as it came up.

The weekend kicked off with a special meal out, with both parents, at a restaurant of the son's choice. At this meal they shared with him what they liked so much about him, and were very specific about the qualities they admired in him. They talked with him about some of the principles they considered important, such as how to treat others and how to conduct yourself in business. They also explained to their son how, over the next few years, they would be giving him more freedoms and choices, as he rewarded their trust.

During the weekend, the eldest son and his dad listened to a set of tapes called *Preparing for Adolescence* from Focus on the Family. There were six tapes, so quite a lot of listening had to be fitted in between BBQ breakfasts, fishing, camping out and other 'boys' stuff. These tapes covered topics such as the physical changes and the social and psychological challenges that young adolescents face: self-esteem, romantic love, ethics and spirituality. After a great weekend, Scott found it interesting that, as they approached home, his son suggested they stop only 100 metres from home to finish listening to the final tape!

By the time son number two was old enough to enjoy his weekend away, there was a set of two tapes called *The Big Weekend* by John Cowan and Jenny Hale. Scott chose these because of their local flavour and because their succinctness suited his 'action-man' second son. Although the two weekends away involved very different activities, (and although Scott decided maybe he had aged in three years!), both were fantastically memorable and invaluable in the understanding that they fostered.

Take the opportunities

In a recent National Campaign to Prevent Teenage Pregnancy poll in the USA, 90 percent of parents said they did not know how to discuss sex with their children. Yet 91 percent of adults and 81 percent of teenagers (aged twelve to nineteen) think that if they could discuss sex with their parents, it would be easier for young people to delay sexual activity and avoid unwanted pregnancy.

Cat Stevens' classic song 'Cat's in the Cradle' hit on a truth when he depicted the earnest son: 'I want to be like you, Dad' and the distracted dad: 'Later son, not now'. There were many opportunities when his boy desperately wanted his dad's time but, in not freely giving it, the father reaped the negative results of living to be a lonely old man, neglected by the very son he had modelled such behaviour to.

ACTION LAB ⟳

TIPS FOR THE MIDDLE YEARS

Monitor your boy's media exposure

We need to protect our boys from becoming brutalised. Over-exposure to violence in an unsupervised atmosphere can expand a boy's capacity for action and rough-and-tumble into violence and cruel behaviour.

Monitor their exposure to violence and cruelty in movies and on television, and don't confuse a boy's natural tendency to play action games (with battles, guns and bombs) with the sadistic violence arising from fear, as a reaction to exposure to gratuitous violence.

Learn how to connect

Have one-on-one 'dates' with your son, enjoying an activity you choose between you, or fun times in a shoulder-to-shoulder activity. If you want to talk, take him for a walk.

Age-appropriate concentration

Ten minutes of chores and ten minutes of reading each night.

Avoid the 'it's not fair' trap

The most common cry of young boys is 'it's not fair'. Parents need to realise that fairness is impossible in every instance. If your boy says 'it's not fair', don't answer with 'well, life isn't fair', otherwise he'll interpret that as 'Mum or Dad aren't fair'. The key is to support the child's emotional need first and then teach the reality of the real world:

Son: It's not fair; Johnnie can go to holiday camp and I can't.

Parent: Well, when you're ten you can go.

Son: But I want to go this year.

Parent: I know it's tough, but two years will fly. Then you can go. Why don't we plan a special day out together for while Johnnie's at camp?

IN SUMMARY 👁

WHAT BOYS NEED DURING THE MIDDLE YEARS

Boys need parents who:

- Take leadership and set clear family rules.
- Create a sense of team in their family.
- Allow for lots of physical activity.
- Offer opportunities to learn skills.
- Listen and talk.
- Train him in values.
- Encourage goals and persistence.
- Support his sport.
- Enforce discipline that is firm and fair.
- Value their son's future healthy sexuality.
- Coach him in healthy 'self-talk'.

Chapter 8

Teenagers – parenting boys in adolescence

A lot of lip service is paid to the modern 'sensitive male' . . .
but the reality is we are surrounded by a popular culture that
is stacked with simplistic, stereotypical and negative images
of masculinity. Everywhere you look there are examples
of violent, impossibly powerful, supermen-type movie
characters, overly aggressive sportsmen and angry, drug-
using, misogynist rock stars.

From a young age, boys are systematically steered
away from their emotional lives towards solitude, silence
and distrust . . . but also at more undetected levels, such
as the 'culture of cruelty' that exists among adolescents,
in which anything a boy says or does can and will be used
against him.

> — *Dan Kindlon and Michael Thompson,* **Raising Cain:**
> **Protecting the emotional life of boys**

Teenagers live in a new world parents cannot yet recognise.
The newness comes from a simple, but striking reality:
seemingly unlimited possibility . . . How does one fashion a
life out of this profusion of opportunities, especially when

there seem to be no penalties for failing? Many . . . become
dazzled and bewildered, frozen by indecision or jabbing
in five directions. A million options promise five million
happinesses, but they often lead to a billion disappointments.

**– *Tim Stafford*, Making Do with More: In an age of
abundance, how do we survive with our souls intact?**

Our world is on a fast-track to change, and both the landscape
for parenting and the ground rules are altering with the ever-
increasing speed of technological development.

A few years ago, I would tell parents to make sure that the computer
was in an area of the house where the screen could easily be seen, so that
you could be in touch with what your teen was looking at on the Internet
and where he was visiting in cyberspace.

But now, if a teenager wishes, he can actually text you out of his life.
The upsurge in mobile phones and their applications has given teenagers
a virtual world of peers that can leave you on the outside, if they wish to
keep you there.

It has also given them a world of options. They can be on their way to
a movie but, through texting each other, within a few minutes the whole
group can decide to change plans and head to a party they just heard
about, a different movie or a mate's place. They tend to be a generation
who keep their options open and the peer group operates in an even more
persuasive way.

Building trust – towards responsibility and independence

It is my belief that, more than any other generation, we parents must
use the years before our sons' puberty wisely. Taking time during these
years to build strong links with our sons and helping to put in place the
building blocks of character which I talked about in the previous chapter
are more important than ever in this new century. The strong links of trust
you build before puberty will be your best ally in remaining part of your

teenage son's life. Trying to be a super-policeman is not a viable option because it will work against the very thing your teenage is looking for from you — respect and trust.

Several recent studies have reaffirmed that the best deterrent still for preventing teenagers from drifting into rebellious and permissive behaviour is that they don't want to let their parents down.

You still have great influence. Even during those first few years of adolescence, when change and challenge seem to be the order of the day and when you may feel your son doesn't even like you, he needs you more than ever to remain relaxed and secure in your role. He may use you as a trusted adult to bounce off, and even kick against, while he is struggling towards independence, but he will thrive so much better if there is a positive atmosphere, appropriate boundaries, two-way communication and a sense that you are progressively giving him more freedom.

So build on the trust you already have, continue to expect the best of him and join the texting network. Send messages of support and interest through texts. This way of communicating is actually a positive. Your teenage son is likely to be super-sensitive to parental communication while with his peers, especially if it involves outward shows of affection. Text messaging avoids this.

HOT TIP ✔

THREE EMPOWERING QUESTIONS

These three questions will help you get to the heart of an issue with your son:

■ What happened?

■ How do you feel about it?

■ What are you going to do about it?

If he merely grunts, try recycling the questions.

First set of answers:

■ Nothing.

■ Lousy.

- Can't do anything.

Repeat the set of questions:

- Coach said I was stupid.
- Real bad.
- I'm not coordinated enough.

Repeat the questions again:

- I think the coach was frustrated with my play.
- I can get over it.
- I'm going to practise more.

Become a pack animal because your teenager is

Just as your teenage son operates as a pack animal with his peers, parents must also have the confidence to act in a pack. Consider taking the initiative and hosting a barbeque or afternoon tea with the parents and classmates of your son at the beginning of the year. This will give you the opportunity to meet the parents and share phone numbers, and to get to know your son's friends.

Remember how you knew almost all your son's friends and their parents at kindergarten? This natural interaction and communication needs to be 'rebooted' during his teenage years. Interestingly enough, parents who have organised some simple event like this have said that their boys and their friends have really looked forward to it. One mother said, 'We parents ended up chatting into the evening while the boys kicked a ball outside or sank some baskets, with the dads joining in.'

Share phone numbers and begin the practice of checking with each other over mundane things like transport and 'picking up' times, while your boys still rely on you in the first year or so of secondary school. This keeps up the connections with other parents — relationships that may be important when something more concerning happens, like a son not arriving home at an agreed time.

HOT TIP ✔

Boys seem to particularly enjoy the sense of belonging to a group. They love the sense of being part of a team and the 'boy company' that their peer group provides. Therefore they are influenced profoundly by their peers, and will often do all sorts of things to be accepted, or will egg each other on when in a group. If possible, having your son belong to several groups outside of school will provide more than one friendship group, such as sporting friends, a youth group or an interest club such a photography, dramatics or music.

What is really going on?

Twice in our lives we experience explosive brain growth over a relatively short period. One is during toddler time and the other happens during — you guessed it — puberty!

Your feisty 'tweenagers' are standing on the same developmental cliff's edge as your toddler was when he threw tantrums and every second word he said was 'No'. They are experimenting with their own autonomy and breaking away from you. However, they don't yet have the brain-power to make good decisions, because they're missing the 'mental traffic cop' that helps most adults sort and compare information before reacting to something. This means that knee-jerk reactions drive most teenagers and toddlers.

Until the last decade, neuroscientists thought the human brain was fully developed by puberty. However, using magnetic resonance imaging technology, they now know that's not true. 'The teenage brain is a work in progress,' says neuroscientist Sandra Witelson in a *US News & World Report* interview. Surprise, surprise!

But here's why this is important. Many of the parenting strategies that fuel great results with toddlers are also perfect for tweenagers. Their brains will only fully mature as parents push them towards making the link between choices and consequences.

HOT TIP ✔

TXT ETIQUETTE

Texting is a great way to communicate, but it needs a framework around it so our children use it respectfully and are treated respectfully in return.

- Establish boundaries around texting. Explain that not everyone can walk straight into your house at any time they want to; you need boundaries for privacy, and to feel safe.
- For the same reason, have zones in your world where you are not accessible electronically.
- Turn your phone off in the movies, at meal times and at bed time.
- It is rude to text, or read texts, while someone is trying to interact with you.
- Don't forget plz and thnk u! Manners can fit in a text!

An attitude of respect

In all your strategies and interactions with your teenage boy there should be an over-riding attitude of respect. All men are looking for dignity and respect. As your son heads into the insecurity of adolescence, a time when he will experiment with his identity and be looking to you for confirmation that he is worthy and acceptable, he needs your affirmation, direction and support to know how to grow.

He needs your motivation, your brains, your adult judgement, your schemes and your dreams. Don't withhold these from your son. You must continue to tell him that he is all right, and back this up with your actions. To be ridiculed is a 'toxic' feeling for men, and teenage boys are particularly vulnerable to ridicule and disrespect. Inspire your son to be honourable. Compliment him, listen to him and keep a sense of humour. People grow into the labels their parents give them.

Unfortunately, the first few years of adolescence can be a roller-coaster for both parents and the boy himself. A son with whom you have always got on easily with may become uncommunicative, tetchy and argumentative, communicating only in grunts. About fourteen years of age is probably the most oppositional time. But this time is made so much worse if he senses that you are still trying to control him and are not working towards allowing him more autonomy. He may feel that he needs to do something drastic to make the point that you are no longer able to control what he thinks and does. You see, now that he is on the other side of puberty, you do have to give up control. Work with the *relationship* you have with your son; his brain is not yet fully mature, but it has turned over from childhood to adolescence.

He is likely to push you away, to question all the things he once accepted from you so readily, and to make some decisions that are totally his own. Driven by his biological clock, he knows that he must individuate and create his own identity, and that means testing your values to decide if he will own or discard them. This is a four- or five-year process, but it will be so much more enjoyable if you work *with* the process and offer your son the respect he craves as he grows.

Let him make decisions, as Barbara Coloroso suggests, as long as they are not physically or morally threatening. Set boundaries on those two bottom lines and allow him to make decisions within those. Let him radically change his hairstyle, paint his bedroom or choose his own clothing. If you don't allow these types of choices, he may make a statement by individuating with alcohol or tobacco — or worse.

Hopefully, the time you have spent building that relationship during the years between six and twelve will all pay off now. Fourteen years of age is actually a window of opportunity to inspire your son towards a positive future. At fourteen, unless they have been abused or are dealing with issues of neglect or drugs, most teenagers have a tremendous sense of possibility about their future. It is now that you can inspire him, fire him with a vision of what he could do and allow him to discover a challenge worthy of his life. Unfortunately, if we ignore this 'window' and allow him to be 'ripped off' by materialism or sexual permissiveness, the window will close and he will settle for that counterfeit satisfaction.

Listen to your son, and support his goals and ideas, wherever possible.

Future focus is a necessity if he is not to get lost in a wilderness of negative boy peer pressure, looking for some nebulous male identity. You will shut down your teenage son if you pontificate and criticise before listening to him. As one boy said, 'My mum's OK, she usually listens to me, but dad just goes on and on.' Communicate the idea that by seventeen years of age he will probably be making just about all of his own decisions but that between now and then there will be many decisions he can negotiate. He will sense the respect behind that sentiment.

If, for example, at age fourteen he wants a tattoo, make a deal with him. Tell him that you are saying no because you don't want him as a thirty-year-old man to look at you and say, 'Why didn't you have the parenting backbone to stop me getting this stupid tattoo! I was only a kid and now I am stuck with it.' Then say, 'However, when you are eighteen, you will be making those sort of choices for yourself.'

HOT TIP ✔

TEENAGE MUSIC

Some teenage music is very dark and pro-suicide. Teenage boys who take their own lives lose perspective. Today nihilism pervades so much of their music — the black desperation of believing nothing has meaning.

Ask your son about the music he likes, the people in the bands, what he thinks is cool, and why.

Ask him if the strong beat (that drives you crazy) is sinister and linked to the negative lyrics — or is it just a beat?

As he is asked to use his judgement, his discernment will grow.

HOT TIP ✔

TEACHING YOUR SON THAT LIFE HAS MEANING AND PURPOSE

Secularism reduces everything to 'thing' and 'function' but life should be underpinned by 'meaning' and 'purpose'.

Start a 'life book' with your boy that shows photos of every stage of his life, holidays, sports events, birthdays, etc. In the difficult teenage years he's likely to open this book and the message he'll get is 'my parents cared enough about me to record my history. I have a past and a future'.

The power of the pack

Teenage boys need big doses of adventure and adrenaline. Joseph Driessen, who has done tremendous work in New Zealand schools with boys, talks about our teenage boys being encouraged into a life that nurtures their masculine spirit. He says they need a structured yet challenging environment: physical activity interspersed with intellectual interests, and positive peer group contact and leadership.

Boys tend to love the male camaraderie of their peers. Therefore, at this age, his group of friends has a profound influence on his behaviour and goals. At a conference of high school principals in Australia, I heard a principal with eighteen years' experience say that even though it is traumatic for a high-schooler to change schools, he would recommend it if your son had friends who were a bad influence on him.

Negative teen peer pressure involves such things as being the biggest and the loudest, one-upmanship, driving fast, being sexually permissive, or drinking till you vomit. Anti-academic peer pressure can squash the joy of achievement. One headmaster said that if boys owned their own cars while they were still at school, it was a sure recipe for losing interest in school, and even led to higher teen pregnancy.

Your son will be different in different groups. Boys mimic each other more than girls do, especially with regards to what they watch and who they hang out with.

On the other hand, those genuine friends your boy makes early in adolescence, through school, sport or other hobbies, will be great allies in his journey, especially if there are mentors as part of the equation. The boys he mixes with at twelve will have a huge influence. Peer pressure peaks at twelve. In fact, if a boy has the same friends from the ages of twelve to sixteen, they are likely to be an influence on each other positively, and even more so if those friendships extend to the parents of those friends. Some of the most positive peer groups I have observed are those where families have been friends and cultivated family friendships through the pre-puberty years.

A group of parents in our suburb have, for several years, organised a monthly 'Whanau Friday' night (Whanau means extended family in the Maori language) for their eleven- to thirteen-year-olds. Two sets of parents are in charge each month, and organise social events which range from ice-skating to a video evening at one of their houses for fifteen to twenty youngsters. This group of young people have gone into their teenage years with a large group of positive friends, as well as good relationships with a group of adults who care about them.

One of the great outcomes of this kind of bonding is that, if your son has good friends at the age of twelve, and they still stick together at eighteen, it will have a powerful influence. For instance, all of them will leave a party together if it gets rough, whereas your son would find that hard alone.

If you don't like the crowd your boy is hanging around with, don't tell him his friends are losers. Introduce others into your family. Go camping with them, have them for sleep-overs and so on. Displace, rather than destroy, friendships.

Take keeping in touch with the families of your teenage boy's friend or friends seriously. For instance, if you drop your teen at another boy's house, just go to the door and introduce yourself and say 'Hi' to the parents. Ask your teenagers for their friends' phone numbers so if you do have worries you can contact them.

If your son is being bullied, it is important for him to be in another group that doesn't have bullies or witnesses to his bullying. In some groups, your boys will find support. Find out where a safe group might be for your boy — perhaps a club where there is a mix of adults as well as boys. He will be a different boy in different groups.

Teenagers and discipline

Silence is an excellent way of letting a boy problem-solve rather than imposing our own solutions. Resist the temptation to make better instantly. Instead of giving advice, rather feed-back on their feelings.

— Ian Lillicoe

Take a hard look at the number and sort of decisions you're making for your kids, then brainstorm how you can give half of them away to your teenagers.

— Foster Cline and Jim Fay

It has been said that we tend to give our children too many instructions, and not enough problems to solve.

Love and logic

Parenting with Love and Logic is a strategy developed by Foster Cline, a psychiatrist, and Jim Fay, a former educator and school principal. It's a treasure trove for parents and builds on the principle that we must create an environment in our homes as close to the real world as possible so that, when we launch our children out into the world, they have a realistic view of how things really work in society.

Natural consequences for good and bad decisions are the best teachers. The best learning experiences you can give your kids stem from giving them significant responsibilities, then not shielding them from the consequences of their decisions (unless life or limb is at stake). The cost of their learning is the cheapest it'll ever be, right now.

Mistakes offer the biggest opportunities for growth. Fay and Cline call the natural consequences that result from bad decisions 'significant learning opportunities'. In fact, they often joke that we should pray for our boys to make mistakes so they will have more opportunities to learn.

We build self-esteem when we give kids responsibility, not when we pound away at them with sweet affirmations. Fay writes, 'The most responsible kids I ever encountered in my three decades in education were the kids at an inner city school where I served as an assistant principal. Those kids woke up in the morning without an alarm clock and got to school in time for breakfast, without any assistance from their parents. They knew that if they got there, they got breakfast; if they didn't, they missed it. Responsible behaviour has a direct correlation to the number of decisions (kids) are forced to make.'

I loved the following email I received after a 'Hot Tips on Parenting Teenagers' seminar, from a mum who tried working to these principles.

> Hello Ian Grant
>
> Thank you again for a very informative evening. Thoroughly enjoyed all that you enlightened me on. I was the one that asked you about my 14, nearly 15-year old boy, regarding him doing his own washing and whether I was actually being reasonable when he has been saying 'that's a mum's job'.
>
> You gave me the courage to carry on the consistency of my discipline that I initiated with regard to him now having to do his own washing as he refused to bring in a dozen items off the line days earlier.
>
> Well, let me tell you, it has worked, but not without its challenges. I came home from work that evening and reinforced my discipline. The child appeared quite happy with this arrangement. Thursday afternoon arrived and I mentioned his washing that still had not been done. He then informed me that his younger sister was going to help him, by doing his washing that he needed for the weekend. Of course I put a stop to that. My son then proceeded to tell me how much of a mother I apparently am not, which I refused to get into an argument about (I did the smile — the thing you recommended

while reinforcing the discipline that I had initially put in place).

However, Friday after school I yet again reminded my son about his washing and how he needed a clean rugby uniform for the next day. After an intensive argument in which I am proud to say that I did not once raise my voice (just did the smile thing) he resorted to telling me that he has not been taught how to use the washing machine so how could he wash his clothes. Well, point taken but I do recall showing him two years prior how this appliance works as he was curious. He did have an argument really as it has been a long time since his first training in clothes washing. However, with my son being so naturally knowledgeable and all, I proceeded to ask him how he installed an alarm system in my car — why, because I didn't know how to; how he can attach mag wheels to my car — why, because I didn't know how to; and how he can pull a stereo apart, fix it and put it back together — why, because I didn't know how to . . . yet he cannot look at a washing machine and work it out!

My poor son had no answer to that . . . I did laugh under my breath and after teaching him step by step how to use the washing machine he finally got his clothes washed. Because I had to go out after he washed his clothes I then txt him reminding him to hang his washing out. After an hour I got home. I noticed his washing on the line . . . Great I thought . . . this has finally sunken in . . . I am not his slave after all . . .

Of course at around 7pm on this Friday I suggested to my son that he bring his rugby uniform in to put it in front of the dehumidifier so it will be dry by the morning. He agreed but unfortunately forgot and I was not going to remind him.

It turns out that the following morning 10 minutes before his game he says to me . . . Oh Mum, I forgot to bring in my uniform like you suggested last night, can I please defrost it in the dryer . . . his uniform was frozen due to the frost we get down here.

Naturally I let him defrost his uniform knowing we had no time to actually have it dry and he was going to wear it wet. My only cost to this could have been a doctor's bill due to him getting the flu . . . fortunately this hasn't happened, but I was prepared to pay that price just to let him know that what I say NOW goes.

My son is now in a regular routine of doing his own washing . . . Oh my God . . . Never thought I'd see this day.

Your seminar was so inspiring . . . and it confirmed that I am doing my parenting job right although I have also realised that there are a few things that I need to brush up on.

Thankful Mum

Connecting their behaviour with its effect on others

Because of their lack of experience and immature frontal lobes, it is normal for teenage boys to be thoughtless, or just not thoughtful. We parents sometimes think that our boys are deliberately punishing us, but usually they have no idea how their behaviour is affecting others.

Another mother explained to me: 'Our teenage boy broke his curfew with the car several times. Each time, he was reprimanded and threatened with loss of use of the car. One night he was really late and had made no explanatory phone call. When he arrived home, we said, "We will talk about this tomorrow." We didn't really trust ourselves not to "lose it" as we were so anxious and angry.

'The next day his father and I were able to talk to him calmly. I went over the family rules. Then I explained how it made me feel when we hadn't heard from him, after the agreed time of his curfew, and what possible outcomes I had imagined. I even told him how long we'd decided to wait before we rang the hospitals. I also stated clearly that it was never, ever too late to ring. (Sometimes boys need things stated very plainly.)

'It was a watershed for our son. It really "clicked" that his actions impacted on us, and he was never late again. Learning how his action had affected the family was far more effective than the threats had been.'

This chapter is not a comprehensive manual on raising teenage boys, as I have already written on that subject in *Parenting Teenagers, the Whitewater Rafting Years* with my colleague John Cowan. But I hope it will give you some useful ideas to put into practice in your family.

HOT TIP ✔

AN ALARM CLOCK CAN BE YOUR ALLY

An alarm clock can be your ally in creating peace of mind when your teenager is out at night.

Set an alarm clock for the negotiated curfew-time of your teenager, and leave it in the hallway. When your teenager arrives home, he turns the alarm off and you are able to sleep through, knowing your child is safe.

If the alarm goes off, you know your teenager is still not home, and you can start finding out where he might be.

Pre-empt discipline issues by building trust

Before your son is due to gain his driving licence, get him to write his own rules for use of the family car. He is likely to write amazingly responsible rules as he proves to you that he can be trusted with your precious vehicle.

But don't just accept his rules automatically. You might suggest some additions, such as filling the tank, cleaning the car, not being on the motorway after 10pm, keeping the law by not driving over the speed limit or taking others when he only has a learner's licence.

HOT TIP ✔

Suggest to your son that he could be setting his own curfew in a couple of years' time. When his ears prick up, explain that you are going to set it now, but every six months that he doesn't break his curfew (unless he calls with a valid reason), you will increase his curfew by half an hour. Explain that if he keeps your trust over the next couple of years, he will then be able to negotiate his own curfew.

Pull the plug on the teenage power struggle

■ *Maintain a united front.* This is most important for issues such as use of the family car, mobile phones, curfews and so on. Sort it out with your spouse first. Agree or disagree in private, but present a united front to your son. Even if your teenage son has limited maths ability he soon works out that two against one is a no-win position.

■ *Learn to negotiate.* Parenting teenage boys is all about making deals. Rules and consequences should be worked out with a teenager, not just dumped on him. A great line to use is 'does that sound fair?'

■ *Don't give way on the non-negotiables.* Clearly state them, and don't budge. Teenage boys loathe wimpy parents.

■ *Tune in.* Strive to understand rather than to be understood. Never say 'in my day'. My father used to say 'I never got the family car when I was young'. I know there were only horses in his day!

■ *Choose your battles well.* You don't have to win every battle, just the important ones. Every good hunter knows that if you take pot shots at the rabbits, you warn off the deer.

Teenage boys and sexuality

> Here's the big word for today — 'dehumanisation' — that's when you go out with someone only for their appearance, their big pecs or their long legs. When you are interested in someone only on the basis of physique, you are dehumanising him or her, seeing that person only as an attractive object. If you are doing that, remember good sex occurs between two human beings, not between two objects . . . and guys, if you exploit a girl, it will come back to get you.
> — *Bill O'Reilly,* The O'Reilly Factor for Kids

When considering your son's teenage years and his journey into manhood, you may feel worried about the sorts of influences he may be exposed to. However, you can relax a little when you remember that half of all happily married people started off as boys! Your son is, or will be, capable of sex (a brief moment of parental shock at that thought is very normal). But even more exciting than that bald statement of biological potential is the reality that your son is also capable of rich and loving relationships, within which sex will be something wonderful and beautiful.

Ultimately it will be his own choices and attitudes that will determine whether sex in his life is something noble and lovely, or dirty and damaged. Parents, though, can improve the odds of happy, healthy sexuality by providing coaching and protection throughout his sexual development.

Sadly, our boys are growing up in an age of 'in-your-face' sexuality, and a society that gives mixed messages with few boundaries. Our culture, in many subtle ways, tends to work against healthy sexuality and future intimacy.

By separating sex from love and commitment, modern culture has disposed with the traditional attitudes which guided young men's behaviour. Ambivalent messages from adults leave our sons without strong guidelines about how and where to set boundaries. This freedom is actually a burden, often leaving them to deal with aggressive sexuality, directed at them from the media, the Internet or needy girls, at a time when their hormones and sexual drives are powerful.

> Boys are often treated one-dimensionally, and ridiculed as being interested in only one thing — sex. However, my experience of teenage boys is that many really value the idea of a good relationship.

A colleague was speaking to a dad in crisis because his thirteen-year-old son had got his thirteen-year-old girlfriend pregnant. This was a really loving dad; a good and caring man who had never expected to find himself in this situation. He said that he had told his boy not to have sex until he was sixteen. However, this was an ambivalent message.

There is a plethora of compelling reasons to put boundaries on sexual intercourse, rather than an arbitrary age limit. Your son must be equipped with those reasons as well as with strong future dreams. Although boys have access to more information than ever before about the biological and contraceptive issues surrounding sexuality, they often hear little about boundaries and future outcomes of sexual choices.

Boys are often treated one-dimensionally, and ridiculed as being interested in only one thing — sex. However, my experience of teenage boys is that many really value the idea of a good relationship. In fact, it is often the boys who say they feel ripped off by being treated as if they only want sex. When speaking at high schools as a now 'older person', after introducing myself and breaking the ice, I often ask if they would allow me to speak to them as a father. I say that we all, as human beings, tend to have two great fears: 'Can I love and will I be loved?' In response, the boys are as thoughtful as the girls. It seems to me that underneath our biology, there are much deeper questions about our worth and the sort of future relationship we hope to build.

These are the sorts of issues surrounding sexuality that, as parents, we can highlight. A recent UK survey showed that faithfully married people tend to be happier, more successful and wealthier. We need to help our boys aim towards rich relationships which will lead to future well-being.

As we often say to high schoolers in our Parents Inc. *Attitude* programmes, 'The important thing is not to wreck the million-dollar future dream with a cheap thrill now. Some choices you could make now will cripple your chances of ever reaching your dream. But there are other choices that will not only lead you in the direction of super sex and intimacy in the future, but will also make the most of today.'

The key is to encourage our sons not to make choices because of the media, the crowd, a poor self-image or on impulse, but to think about the level of friendships they want to enjoy before they commit to an eventual long-term relationship. The very boundaries that they set on their sexuality will actually allow them far more opportunity to enjoy and explore friendships with girls, at a level that is safe, creative and allows them to back out with fewer complications than if sex was involved.

Here's an interesting fact: in 2003, the US National Campaign to Prevent Teen Pregnancy learned from polling 1,000 teenagers that roughly nine out of ten teens believed that open, honest conversation with their parents would help them postpone sex until the right time.

HOT TIP ✔

One of the most potent influences in a boy's formation of attitudes towards women will be his father's attitude toward his mother, and his mother's respect for herself.

When we tell married people that 'sex begins in the kitchen', we mean that sex is about so much more than just the physical act. It is also about the many other dimensions of the relationship — how to get on with others, how to express love through actions, how to communicate, to use manners, to be thoughtful and to see their sexuality as the ultimate expression of love. The best way, of course, is to do this by modelling kindness, love, self-sacrifice and thoughtfulness in our daily actions and reactions as parents.

But teenagers also need information. They need to know that love comprises many different elements — friendship, trust, spirituality and physical expression among them — and that all must come together in true human intimacy. Tragically, our modern society often puts the physical aspect ahead of the other elements. I tend to think that the area of most dishonesty in human communication is usually about sexuality.

Respect

An overriding attitude of respect, for oneself and others, is the best fertiliser for good sexual growth. With boys, this needs to be taught through giving clear expectations of behaviour towards others.

Coach them on polite phrases and good manners, which are essential ways of showing respect (and ultimately an awesome skill to use in the pursuit of a mate!). Curb critical and disparaging comments, even if the other person can't hear them — 'How would you feel if that was your sister or your mother?'

Boys need to be rescued from overlaying sex with a patina of grubbiness. Parents can monitor limits of humour, media content and conversation. Say 'No, that topic is too precious and special to be spoken about like that' or 'You've got a great sense of humour. You can be really funny without having to use grubby humour like that.'

The 'feelings-based', non-directive model for sex education used in many schools has huge limitations and in some cases has contributed to the sexual chaos which leaves our kids floundering for a framework. New Zealand's level of abortions, teenage pregnancies and STDs (among the highest in the world), for example, show that teenagers need more than just the basic factual information.

Dr William Coulson, one of the original designers of this therapy-based, non-directive sex education, which was developed in the 1960s when 'feelings-based' therapy was at its height, later repudiated the whole idea of treating sex education this way. He regrets the experiment, asserting how inappropriate this model was for teenagers. In his words, 'Teenagers don't need therapy, they need direction.'

You would never give the keys of the latest high-powered sports car to a twelve-year-old, asking him to make his own decisions about what speed to drive at. The risk of him crashing and burning is huge. The ever-present factor with teenagers is that they tend to think they are bullet-proof. This is healthy in some ways, but in the area of sexuality it can be dangerous. I often joke when talking to high-school-aged boys that, if they were down in the valley with their girlfriend and her father was on top of the hill with a high-powered rifle saying 'If anyone touches my daughter, I'll shoot him', you would think, 'He could miss!'

While understanding the huge role that testosterone has in our son's biological make-up, and the reality of how that shapes his view of the world, we must also accept his ability to love deeply and to commit to a journey of faithful relationships.

Our Parents Inc. website, www.attitude.org.nz, is a creative and humorous site designed for teenagers. It will challenge their thinking and encourage them to carefully assess their decisions in this area.

What information do you give?

In conclusion, yes — they will probably get lots of information from school. No — they will not get enough, and it may not be early enough to head off the flood of misinformation that circulates the schoolyards or pours out of the TV. 'The book left on the bed' is a good introduction to the topic, but it needs a follow-up talk. Remember to give the clear message, 'It is okay to talk to me about these topics.' *The Big Weekend* CD, which we talked about earlier, or 'Sex with Attitude' from our Parents Inc. website are both useful resources.

Whether you are a mother parenting on her own or a two-parent family, mothers have a big role to play in communicating information. Your admiration for your son, your respect for yourself, and your instincts will be a great guide. Friends and relatives may help by modelling respectful talk and relationships, and may even involve your son in their family rituals, but you will need to find good information for your son if you are doing it on your own.

If your son does have a book with good information, that will be a foundation for his knowledge and your conversations. Books like *'What's Happening To Me?'* by Peter Mayle or *Secret Men's Business — Manhood, the Big Gig* by John Marsden may be useful. Like the father and son camping trip we talked about earlier, a mother can also listen with her son to *The Big Weekend* CD (order from www.parentsinc.org.nz) together while driving. It will allow you to listen together without having to make eye contact, which can be helpful if either of you are self-conscious.

Specific issues
Wet dreams and masturbation

Much of today's literature would tell you that masturbation is a universal and harmless behaviour among teenage boys and men. However, there are issues to consider in the overall picture of your son developing future healthy relationships. With young teens, the issue of masturbation is more of biologically induced urgency than morality, but it becomes a different issue later, where it can impact on relationships. People who opt for the easy gratification of masturbation sometimes fail to devote their energy to developing intimacy and mature lovemaking.

What is a big deal is the risk of masturbation becoming a habit, and its association with pornography and sexual fantasy. Boys need to learn to not only curb their sexual behaviour but also to put limits on their sexual thought-life. Imagining illicit sex does not automatically lead to sexual misbehaviour, but it almost always precedes it. It is a rehearsal of selfish sex, where the end is self-gratification. Mature love is outwardly focused and 'other-person' centred. Selfish love is 'me-centred' and concerned with only meeting your own needs.

The best advice to boys is, if they do masturbate, not to get too hung up about it. They should see it as an immature thing, very much associated with a stage when hormonal drives are at their strongest.

Talk about wet dreams as well, which don't happen to all boys, and will probably not occur until they are thirteen or fourteen years of age. Again, the word you need to get across is 'normal'. The dreams that accompany the nocturnal emission are normally pleasant, but occasionally disturbing. Reassure your boy: dreams are the brain wheel-spinning, and usually signify nothing at all.

Hygiene

Teenage boys' behaviour can range from a Neanderthal ignorance of soap and water to a neurotic obsession with toiletries and grooming. Your son may need specific advice on how much and when: aftershave is a nice touch but he doesn't need to marinate in it; a clean shirt every day is fine, but not three times a day. And he may need to be reminded that toiletries are no substitute for hygiene — multiple layers of deodorant do not obviate the need for a shower.

HOT TIP ✔

Feed-back positive comments, especially as your son develops the 'glass ego' of adolescence. 'Your hair looks great!' 'Hey, look at you!' 'Mmmm . . . that's a nice fragrance . . . is that your deodorant?' 'I wish I still had enough hair to do that!'

Dating

For some boys, dating won't be a serious issue until their late teens but, driven by the media and our culture, it is becoming a significant issue for many at a much younger age.

Who's going out with who? is already a major feature of conversation among early and pre-teens. Admittedly, it is often the girls who are driving the 'going out' phenomenon at this early stage, but it's the boys who are their objects of interest. Girls are now expected to be more aggressive in their romances: they are much more forward in making approaches to boys, by texting, writing notes and making phone calls.

'Going out' might not mean they actually go anywhere — it may just mean walking home together or sitting near each other at school, or even nothing at all. For others, it means a lot more than just going somewhere — some estimate that 10 percent of girls have had sex in their early teens, usually with boys who are a lot older.

Parents tend to worry less about their boys dating than about their girls, possibly because boys don't get pregnant! But boys need to know that there are limits, responsibilities and skills.

Many parents who grew up in the 1960s and 1970s have no clear boundaries or expectations of their teenagers except to tell them to wear a condom. But, as a parent, you have a duty to give your child the best chance of a great future. Being a teenage father, or having to face an abortion or STD (sexually transmitted disease), or the angry parents of a girlfriend, are all experiences your son does not need. Even if your son shows some responsibility and uses a condom, they have a notoriously bad record of failure when used by inexperienced teenagers.

It is far better to give him a future dream, and to coach him into setting boundaries on his friendships during his teenage years. As I said earlier, a boy who sets boundaries on his sexuality has a much better chance of exploring multi-dimensional friendships and being creative about those friendships and dating. The opportunity to enjoy many safe friendships with girls will give him a much better idea of the sort of person that he will choose as a life-companion in later years.

Teenagers of all ages should have clear limits regarding the time they are expected home, and where they are going. With older boys, it will be their own standards and values that do the chaperoning. Inspire your boy to have a high respect for himself, women in general and his date in particular. Your teenager will not be getting encouragement to be cautious or celibate from the media, schools, authorities or their mates — in fact, the overwhelming message our culture gives young people is 'Go for it!' Your voice might seem like a thin, wavering squeak against the roar of competing sexual messages but, because you are his parent, it will still be very powerful.

Ninety percent of teenage relationships fail within a year — and the pain is very real afterwards, to the point that some boys become depressed (boys can be very negatively affected by break-ups). When a break-up happens, take it seriously. Your comfort and reassurance can be very important.

Model courtesy and respect if you are honoured with meeting your son's girlfriend. Some parents never get that privilege, mainly because their sons are afraid their parents will embarrass them!

If you find yourself in a situation where a girl is not expecting to go home, and assumes it is OK with you that she stays over, you can still show kindness to the girlfriend but you do not need to change your values. Most teenage sex is actually enabled in some way by parents. 'You may sleep with your girlfriend when you can supply the bed, the roof and handle any consequences.' Politely explain that you have a spare bed for visitors and that you have an open-door policy for bedrooms when friends are around. Make sure you put on a great breakfast and enjoy sitting around as a family, getting to know the new 'friend'.

A mother is important

Maternal advice and reassurance is our gift to our sons in this area. Boys need their mothers to teach them about relationships, and to model and encourage the softer aspects of life. As Steve Biddulph says in *Raising Boys*, 'They need their mothers to bless and enjoy their masculinity and to offer positive, affirming ideas about boys and men.' (Read the chapter on the value of mothers again, for how they play such a crucial role in successfully getting boys through the teenage years.)

Pornography

Parents have to realise that today's pornography is not like the 'girlie' magazines we used to peek at when we were at school. It's like comparing shandy with brandy; today's pornography is nerve-jarring stuff.

Where do most young teenagers get their first taste of pornography? These days it is likely to be on the Internet. It has been estimated that 65 percent of graphic images on the Internet are pornographic, and that 300 new pornographic sites are added daily. Even innocent searches will sometimes bring up pornographic sites.

Apart from the useful strategy of blocking these sites at source, by using an appropriate filter, teach your sons to wrap boundaries around stuff they may be exposed to. Teach them to say to themselves, 'I will just never go there; it is not worth the future fallout.'

Most good standards derive from principles of love and respect, and pornography is an offence against human dignity. Pornography degrades women and robs men, giving them a one-dimensional view of women. The fantasy ideals of pornography can rob people of truly satisfying relationships.

If you find pornography in your son's room or on his computer, confrontation in a caring manner is the best method. It may be helpful to share, from your own experience, the sexual drives and temptations you faced as a teenager. This puts you in a more vulnerable position but, by being more honest with your teenager, chances are you will be more effective. If you can evoke his empathy, he is more likely to hear your point of view and not want to disappoint you. (You can also be honest about the sad outcomes of destroyed marriages and the destruction of intimacy through pornography.)

Expect good things of your boys. Have dreams for their relationships and encourage them to have dreams for themselves. Talk about the difference between sex and love. Appeal to their idealism about the future and their self-respect.

HOT TIP ✔

EQ or emotional intelligence, as apposed to IQ, is defined by psychologists as the ability to:

■ Communicate with others.

■ Empathise with others.

■ Delay gratification until the task is completed.

Teenage boys with good EQ will become those of whom you are most proud in the years to come.

Building resilience in your boys

A *Harvard Business Review* research paper stated 'More than education, more than experience, more than training, a person's level of resilience will determine who succeeds and who fails. This is true in the cancer ward; it's true at the Olympics; and it's true in the boardroom.'

Their conclusions about resilience are that it is based on three things.

■ Hope based on reality.

■ Meaningfulness in life.

■ Innovative survival.

Humour, warm support and coaching in healthy self-talk will build this resilience.

A teenage boy might tell himself: 'It's going to last forever.'

A parent says: *'This is now; it's not forever.'*

'It's going to affect everything I do.'

'This affects something but not everything.'

'The pain is bad; I can't cope.'

'The pain is bad but you can *cope.'*

I'm always fascinated by the story of the three armed forces recruiters who spoke to senior students at a high school in the United States. The total time allotted was forty-five minutes, and the representative of each branch of the armed forces was given fifteen minutes. After a toss of a coin, it was decided that the Army representative would go first. But he got carried

---

HOT TIP ✔

FIVE WAYS TO PROMOTE RESILIENCE IN YOUR SON

- Boys need adults who are charismatic in their lives. This makes a boy feel safe, valued and listened to. They need someone from whom they can draw strength.
- Develop his emotional and social competencies, such as:
  - Anger management.
  - Decision making.
  - Problem solving.
  - Empathy for others.
- The family as a team gives a boy a great sense of:
  - Meaning.
  - Purpose.
  - Belonging.
- Coach his self-talk. Positive self-talk underlines optimistic teenage boys.
- Develop islands of competence in their lives so they feel secure and receive praise from other adults.

---

away and talked for twenty-one minutes. Not wanting to be outdone, the Air Force representative spoke for twenty-three minutes. The final speaker, a Marine sergeant, knew he had only two minutes before the bell would shatter the boys' concentration. He rose to the podium and, for one and a half minutes, he eyed each boy in the auditorium. Every student sensed his piercing gaze. Then he said, 'I reckon two or three of you will make it in the Marine Corps. I'd like to talk to you in the cafeteria after the bell.' You've guessed it — he had a huge queue of boys lining up to see him.

That Marine sergeant had worked with men long enough to know that their deepest desire is to be challenged and respected.

Decisions from the chest

How does a man make a decision? Boys can be made aware that there are three types of decisions they can make: mind (rational), chest (manly) and lower body (physical, passionate).

Throughout the history of the human race, people have understood the need to get men to make decisions in their chests. C. S. Lewis once wrote a great essay called 'Men Without Chests', in which he pilloried modern men as being driven by their lower passions (the base drives of food, sex, survival) or by their rational minds.

The prestigious Harvard Business School once tested its graduating accounting students by placing the following scenario in front of them: 'If you could commit corporate fraud for a large sum of money, and you knew you would never be caught, would you do it?' A staggering 95 percent said they would. The school panicked and immediately introduced ethics courses. These students were making decisions in their minds or bellies, not in their chests.

In our chests we make the really big choices of life: what do I believe, what do I value, where will I be loyal, what is my duty, how shall I practise discipline? In the movie *We Were Soldiers*, we get a glimpse of why the military teaches men to make decisions in their chests, not in their minds or their stomachs.

No one will rationally charge down a machine gun nest; nor will he do so if he relies on the feelings in his stomach. But a man will do so if he believes that there is a higher call to be answered, a summons that comes from his chest — where his beliefs and mettle are tested.

What we have to instil into boys is a desire to be great men; to know how, when and why to sacrifice for others, and to understand discipline. Reading books about great men who make tough moral decisions, like Shackleton, in the book *Survival*, may just be the trick.

HOT TIP ✔

Tell your son that he's like an author who's writing a book: each person is writing their life story. He's born into chapter 2. (Chapter 1 is about his heritage and roots.)

If he feels he is in a bad chapter, where things have gone wrong, let him know that it is OK to acknowledge that he has made mistakes and that he can learn to deal with the past, mentally close the chapter and begin a fresh chapter in his life story.

Life is not a book that just happens. He has an active role as the author.

Loving your teenager

It is easy to love babies. Even when they're puking down the back of your shirt, they are inherently lovable. But then they grow — it can be a lot harder to love adolescents.

My colleague John Cowan says, 'I've seen it on numerous wildlife programmes — the young wildebeest, or bear cub, or gosling, or whatever, is eventually pushed away by its mother and out of the family circle. I'm not a biologist, and the programmes don't actually show this, but I imagine that this happens when the young animal starts running up huge phone bills, listens to loud awful music and talks back to the head of the herd with a sassy smart mouth.'

Teenagers go through a stage when they are hard to love and yet, according to the American Academy of Child and Adolescent Psychiatry, communicating love to your child is the *single most important* thing you can do. This is because your teenagers decide how they feel about themselves in large part by how you react to them; and those feelings have a huge impact on their behaviour and the decisions they make. Some of those decisions could have a lifetime of consequences, such as attitudes about work, study, sex, alcohol, drugs and so on.

Your love might not be reciprocated, at least in the short term. If you want guaranteed loyalty, love, respect and affection, maybe you should buy a dog, because there may well be a period when you get precious little of it from your teenager. You will need to show grace: the virtue of extending love even if it is not responded to. Persevere though, and you will be rewarded with a happier home, less stress, and a lifelong loving relationship with your child.

Nothing severs communication with a teen more quickly than parental anger. Emotional over-reaction tends to cause an adolescent to respect the parent less. How can you expect good self-control from your teenager if you do not have it yourself?

If you were to graph the amount of affectionate touching a child receives as he grows, you would see that babies get heaps of cuddles and kisses. That physical affection reduces through the preschool years, drops off even more (especially for boys) during primary school and often completely vanishes at adolescence. There are probably many young teenagers who aren't being touched by anyone. It is no wonder then that so many teens fly into early and inappropriate sexual behaviour — they are touch-starved. True, many teenagers won't want to be kissed or hugged by their parents, especially anywhere within five miles of the school gate, but that is often just a stage. If you haven't had a hug with your teenager lately, why not give it a try. If you get the cold shoulder, the stage isn't over! It might be safer to just rest a hand on their shoulder, or tousle their hair, or massage a sore muscle or scratch their back.

HOT TIP ✔

TAKE ADVANTAGE OF TECHNOLOGY

Mobile phones can be a source of conflict, especially when it comes to negotiating who pays for them. Turn that around.

- If your teenage son wants a mobile phone, tell him he must come up with a financial plan that he can work with.
- It's often embarrassing for a teenage boy to answer phone calls from his mum, but you can text him. He can answer you without his mates knowing.

- Mobile phone curfews are important for family survival. A great rule is for everybody to put their phone in the basket in the kitchen at 8pm. It stays there until the morning (this is a good practice for parents too).

ACTION LAB 🔁

TIPS FOR PARENTING TEENAGERS

Here are a few ways you might like to try to show your love:

- *Invite your teenager's friends to your house for pizza, soft drinks and a DVD. (Extra points if you can secure a big-screen TV or video projector.)*
- *Let your teenage boy open his own account, and allow him to do his own shopping for clothes and other necessities. He will learn responsibility, self-control and the value of money.*
- *What are the positives about your teenager? Why not roll them into a genuine, unqualified compliment and give it to him.*
- *Grit your teeth, force a smile, and ask your teenager to play his favourite music to you. Discuss the music with him and find out why he likes it so much. Recover from this bonding session by listening to an entire Beatles double album!*
- *Get better at loving your spouse. Teenagers respond to the emotional atmosphere in the home. If there is bickering or tension between parents they will respond to that, often in an immature way. They may avoid being at home, or 'punish' their parents for their behaviour. A secure relationship between parents makes teenagers feel secure.*

IN SUMMARY 👁

WHAT YOUR TEENAGE BOY NEEDS

Your teenage boy needs:

- Trust and opportunities to show responsibility.
- Opportunities to pit himself against challenges, physical and intellectual.
- Big doses of adventure and adrenalin.
- Positive peer groups.
- Respect from parents who believe he has 'what it takes'.
- A positive atmosphere, appropriate boundaries and great communication.
- Parents who will link choices with consequences.
- The opportunity to make mistakes and learn from them.
- A respectful attitude towards his own sexuality, and clear goals for future relationships.
- Strong beliefs that create resilience.
- Parents who will enable his journey towards manhood.

Chapter 9

Mastering competence, confidence and initiative

If every parent sat on the end of their child's bed at night and debriefed about their day, 90 percent of my work as a therapist would be unnecessary.

— Dave Riddell, therapist and seminar speaker

Children are, as a rule, very good observers but poor interpreters of life's happenings. They need loving adults to interpret for them. Consequently, parents must make a deliberate commitment at night to sit at the end of the bed with their boy, allowing him to 'empty the pockets' of his day and chat with him about what's going on for him. This is your opportunity to enter his world, to enjoy it together, and, if necessary, to interpret it for him from an adult's perspective.

Bad behaviour is usually sourced in bad moods, and bad moods are usually the result of bad self-talk.

I was always pleasantly surprised, when walking down the hallway after bedtime, to hear one of our teenage boys call out 'Hey Mum', or 'Hey Dad', 'Would you come and sit on my bed, there's something I need to talk to you about.' As our children became young adults, I was honoured when they would occasionally call up and say 'Hey Mum and Dad, can I come over for a meal — there's something I'd like to run past you.'

Where did this sense of trust and sharing start? It began with the routine chat and debrief on the end of the bed that had always been part of our day. It was a tradition and we were all nurtured by it. Over the years this tradition had far bigger pay-offs than we had ever imagined when we began it with our toddlers.

Give him the gift of your 'eyes'. This proactive, positive attention, given with love, is invaluable. It is an opportunity for you to give perspective to a child's interactions during the day, to coach him in friendship or to give him skills to cope. Lend him your 'eyes' and your adult wisdom and support as he is negotiating and interpreting his daily experiences.

As the result of a painful experience, a child will often take on a wrong belief that could affect him for the rest of his life. If this painful experience leads him to a false conclusion about his value or worth, it may cause stress, anxiety and anger for him throughout his life

A myriad of childhood experiences have the potential to set up a boy who doesn't have an available adult for future pain. Noises in the night, bullying at school, or even something that may appear trivial to an adult, such as not having the money for a book or trip at school, can all set up children for painful wrong beliefs, such as: 'The world is a dangerous place', 'Something terrible will happen if I make a mistake or let somebody down', 'I will be abandoned or get rejected if I don't achieve'.

When we don't have a loving adult in our lives, we tend to create our own reality. Then we may protect that reality for the rest of our lives, using anger or moodiness.

If life is to be savoured, we need to process the bad times and celebrate and enjoy the good times. If your boy hears something during the day that confuses or puzzles him, you can interpret. If he has done something dumb, you can help him avoid ongoing unnecessary guilt and self-blame by talking together through a solution, and supporting him with a new skill or insight.

> It is important to teach your boy into a reality that he can live with, rather than a delusion that oppresses him.
>
> — *Dave Riddell*, Living Wisdom

It is your loving coaching that will give your boy a more realistic 'reading' of a situation, as well as equipping him with ideas and skills in dealing with it. If a boy is to tell himself the truth, he needs to hear it from an adult first.

You need to explain that 'failure isn't fatal — we just need to try again, but maybe with some new skills'. Or give him a message such as, 'Our value and worth is not in other people's hands.'

I personally wish that this had been my experience as a young boy. Because of a childhood stutter, and the lack of parental 'debriefing' (even though my parents loved me and worked hard to find an answer to my stutter), I carried misbeliefs for years about my value and worth. It was only years later, when the wheels began to fall off the corners of my marriage, that I discovered what was really happening. These hidden, childhood misbeliefs sabotage us subconsciously and warp our perceptions.

So, talking around the dinner table, in a safe way, listening to each child, allows you as the 'big person' to realign their perspectives, to teach them to tell themselves the truth. Helping your child laugh about a situation may be the answer, or helping them develop verbal skills which will deflect others' mockery and create a joke. Other family members may join in and contribute suggestions.

Teasing and 'put-down' culture

If your boy is being mocked or put down, you might like to show him how to reverse the 'tease' by agreeing with the mocker, and creating a humorous twist. He can subtly show those around them that the arrows of mocking are not penetrating their target.

For example:

'Who taught you to play soccer? Your Grandma?'

'Yes, actually Granny did. She had some pretty good moves for a ninety-two-year-old!'

'You've got the biggest nose in the class. We call you "hose nose"!'

'I'll have you know this nose is in the Guinness Book of Records!'

(You may like to find a copy of *Sticks and Stones* by Scott Cooper for more great ideas.)

If parents deliberately debrief with their son each day, they will avoid wrong beliefs and attitudes developing in their son's future.

> If a child goes to sleep on a wrong belief,
> He will wake up with a wrong conclusion.
> If he goes to bed with a wrong conclusion,
> He will wake up with a wrong mood.
> If he goes to sleep on a wrong mood,
> He'll wake up with a wrong attitude.
> If he goes to sleep with a wrong attitude,
> He'll wake up, as an adult, with a wrong character.
> If he goes to sleep with a wrong character,
> He'll wake up with a wrong destiny.

I have often invited Dave Riddell, a therapist and seminar speaker, to be a guest on my radio show. I am always impressed how, in those real-life and revealing encounters on air, men who would never visit a counsellor for help, poured out their hearts. It is no mean feat to get men talking about their issues. I'm convinced that it has been his practical, technical and straightforward approach that so often has got right to those things which have been affecting men and their families. At the root of what he believes is that we must have the truth in any situation to help us to live healthily. He offers people 'truth coaches' to help them realign a belief that they have held for decades.

We parents can become 'truth-coaches' for our boys. A boy who is disappointed and in despair, can be gently told that 'No doesn't mean never', or 'Not now doesn't mean never.'

It's important that parents use empowering questions as they probe to discover the real issue. For example, 'Well, I know it's horrible, and you feel yuck, but I wonder if your feelings could be telling you lies? Perhaps it's not a disaster to be nicknamed; perhaps it's only uncomfortable. After all, life isn't a popularity contest is it? Mum and I think you're the coolest kid anyone could have, so that's what really matters — and we've known you all your life.'

It is amazing how one 'truth' will be a depth-charge of confidence for your son. Boys' brains, especially, are structured for bullet-point information. They don't like us to 'go on and on', but a quick bullet point will give them something to hang on to for the rest of their lives. A number of 'bullet points' that still operate in my head are those I learnt in my childhood:

- 'Every problem has a solution — you've just got to find it.'
- 'Play as fairly and work as hard as if all the world were looking on.'
- 'A good night's sleep finds the answers to a lot of problems.'

Taking a boy 'out of the mainstream' does not necessarily protect him as effectively as a listening ear, insight and empowerment. It is 'truth' that keeps him safe. Having said that, there will be situations when a boy is drowning, or has really negative peers, in which wise parents will know he needs respite or a different environment and will act decisively.

HOT TIP ✔

TEACH YOUR BOY THE POWER OF CHOICE

The three components we have to work with are our genes, our circumstances and our choices.

He can't do much about his genes; he has his dad's nose and his mum's eyes. Until he's older he can't do too much about his circumstances. But he can learn early to make good choices.

Success in life is 10 percent what happens to us, and 90 percent what we do about it.

Self-worth and parental support

Boys deal with correction so much more positively when their self-worth is secure. We have the great privilege of supporting our child, giving him the beliefs and reassurance that he is a worthwhile human being, and equipping him with the resources and back-up to handle what life throws at him.

Remember Dr Timothy Stuart, author of *Raising Children at Promise*, who saw hundreds of children battle major adversity, but succeed, because of a caring mentor. Testosterone has less effect on a boy than the way he is loved, nurtured and shaped by his parents.

In his book, *The Optimistic Child*, Dr Martin Seligman suggests that, when children learn helplessness, it is not just because bad things happen to them. It is because they think they can do nothing about those bad things. He describes an experiment with dogs that got him thinking — researchers gave dogs electric shocks, and were amazed to find that, even though they could have moved away from the shock the dogs didn't, because they decided they couldn't do anything to stop the shock. 'We found that we could cure helplessness by teaching animals that their actions had effects. We could prevent learned helplessness by providing early experience at mastery.'

We are often tempted to praise our boys so they feel better, when in reality their effort is mediocre. We'll say 'That's amazing', but our boy knows it isn't. As a parent-coach, this is when teaching good 'self-talk' can counter our boy's habit of not giving his best. One of my grandsons becomes frustrated easily when he can't immediately master a new skill. His parents tell him, 'You have done so well for someone who is five. Even bigger boys find that hard. Let's keep trying, because you will learn in a day or two.'

A 'can do' attitude, coached by an affirming parent, will help a boy interpret failures and grow in competence.

Mastery and helplessness

We can inoculate boys against depression by giving them a sense of mastery over their own lives: a sense that they can take action and it will make a difference.

'Learned helplessness' comes from believing 'I can't do anything about what is happening to me'. This attitude leads to passivity and pessimism. Pessimism colours a boy's whole attitude towards life. It results in an entrenched habit of mind that leads to resignation and under-achievement.

The inner-directed boy believes that life events are largely the result of his choices and are therefore his responsibility. This gives a boy a sense of ownership and power over his life that will enable him to accept the unchangeable yet work to improve and alter his circumstances where possible. He will have strong values, goals and persistence.

Boys like this have been allowed to negotiate with their parents and make changes that will allow them to pursue their goals. For example, a friend of mine turned down his eleven-year-old's son's request for a mobile phone. However, he made the offer that, if his son gathered a number of prices and came up with a business plan for how he was going to finance the ongoing use of a mobile, he would reconsider. His son went away, did his research and concluded himself that he couldn't afford the operating costs at the moment. This process left the boy's dignity intact, and reconfirmed a respectful, ongoing relationship with his dad that left room for negotiation and success.

We often confuse knowledge with wisdom

Boys who have not had strong messages about their own capability to influence change could be labelled 'outer directed'. These kids tend to think that life circumstances are largely the result of chance or luck, rather than choice. They are less likely to be willing to see change as positive, because they feel powerless to alter the circumstances of life. Ultimately they will see themselves as victims. Inner-directed boys, on the other hand, have much more satisfying and happier lives, because they see choices and changes as being within their power.

ACTION LAB

TIPS FOR CONNECTING

■ Be available to coach your son in his inner life, handing on wisdom and, where necessary, truth by debriefing. Always be unshockable. Learn to say 'Mmm, anything else?' 'What do you think about that?' Build trust – let your son know you are on his side against the problem.

■ Proactively build times into your schedule to connect with your son Your aim is to build genuine friendship that will see you through the rough patches.

■ Manage the media. Sit down with your son – nothing beats watching movies with your son, asking him what he learned, or commenting on violence when it is graphic. Michael Gurian, in The Wonder of Boys, suggests that you create a chart and get your boy to write down his favourite movies. Ask him what he liked and what he didn't about each one. What did he learn? What did he think was realistic and could really happen? What did he think was an unlikely outcome? Ask him about the violence, whether it was gratuitous or OK in context. Ask him if he would be happy watching the movie with his mother or his sister.

Chapter 10

Boys and masks – talking to the real boy

> Our home can become a haven of peace for our children,
> who may have faced conflict at school and elsewhere.
> At home we can give our children space to unwind and
> the gift of protection from mocking or insult.
>
> *— Christine Day*

I recently spoke at a conference for educators in Perth, Australia, on the subject of boys and the specific challenges that educating them in our western culture brings. I sat in on a session where the speaker, fresh from a Churchill Fellowship in the UK, communicated some interesting insights on the tendency of boys to wear 'masks' when they feel misunderstood, inadequate or threatened.

At the discussion following the lecture, this group of experienced educators discussed strategies for addressing this phenomenon of 'mask wearing'. One high school principal said when dealing with a staunch, rebellious boy, he would always know that the key to making progress was to speak to the boy behind the mask and give him dignity. He would say something like, 'In my office, no one wears masks. I'm going to take mine off and I want you to remove yours, so we can talk man to man.'

Within the spectrum of 'boyness' there are personalities that range from impulsive and brave to sensitive and timid, but there is also an emotional vulnerability about boys that we must protect. Just as the knights of old protected themselves with a suit of armour, many boys don a metaphorical mask in order to cope with the daily battles of living and the challenges of being accepted by their peers.

Why do boys feel they need to hide who they really are? It is often because they don't feel acceptable or good in their true masculine identity. A boy will often feel safe behind a mask, using it to protect himself from ridicule or feelings of inferiority.

Many of our teenage boys feel soft inside, yet their brain tells them they are meant to be strong — capable of protecting and providing for those they care about. They reach inside for their manliness but only discover 'marshmallow', the result of not being modelled into masculinity. So they develop masks to give themselves the appearance of toughness, staunchness or coolness. Teenage boys put up a front to protect their real selves such as a one-dimensional macho image picked up from the movies or older boys. To some teenage boys, gangs are attractive because they offer a collective mask, and a place where they feel accepted. Others put on a mask as protection against bullying, or to avoid showing their true emotions. This can happen with teenage boys and their mothers: 'You can't make me do it!' 'So what!' 'This is so boring!'

Masks such as humour or flippancy help them to appear cool when breaking the 'peer group' rule.

However, in order to truly communicate, to understand and be understood, our masks need to be lowered. Masks between parent and child, teacher and pupil, boss and worker, as well as between men and women, inhibit communication and promote misunderstanding. If a boy is to really grow and understand himself, he needs to be able to step out from behind the mask and be his true self. We need to show boys that they are acceptable and whole without their masks, and to communicate that it takes courage to put the mask down.

This issue has become especially pronounced for boys in our culture because of the lack of coordinated community responsibility for boys. Previous generations in many cultures would take boys at puberty and accept them into the manhood club through specific initiations which often involved a hurdle to conquer. In this way they affirmed the boy, communicating, 'You are now a man-apprentice and we will mentor you towards manhood, teaching you how to be a man.'

Because we often don't have these community traditions any more, parents need to create them for their teenage sons.

We can give our son confidence so that he doesn't need a mask because his masculine soul is developing to maturity. To speak to the mask is to give it validity. The challenge for us as parents is to also take off our own masks as we encourage our teenage boys to do the same. Only then will we be really communicating.

On a recent phone-in radio show on this subject, a father rang and confessed that he sometimes puts on a mask of anger when he arrives home tired, as he wants his children to obey quickly. So, as parents, we may need to take the initiative, to take the risk of practising more openness and vulnerability, by taking off our own masks. Then we can encourage our boys to do the same.

Avoid confrontations with your mask-wearing son in front of other children — particularly if he is the eldest, as this will give him a macho badge to wear that reads 'I can stand up to Mum or Dad'. Instead, when a confrontation begins, quietly say, 'We need to talk about this, one on one,' or 'We'll talk about it later.' Then later, when things have cooled down, take him for a walk or talk to him in private. Say something like, 'Son, when we are together we need to take off our masks and talk man to man.'

For mothers, I suggest a different approach. Choose a time when you can be alone, or create one, then say something like, 'Ben, you are a better boy than this', 'This isn't like you', or 'How can we work it out?' Be prepared to negotiate.

To allow him to come out from behind his mask and show his real self, ensure that there is some male authority in his life to whom he is accountable. This may be his dad, but it may also be his school teachers, a sports coach, youth leader, a boss at his after-school job, or his granddad.

Give him tasks that are part of the family rules and that require communal compliance and performance. Family chores are not just an added extra; they perform the task of making a boy feel significant and a vital member of the family team. The chores can be more extensive and responsible the older he becomes.

ACTION LAB ♺

TIPS ON MASKS

Boys won't feel the need to wear a mask when they are part of a positive peer group.

Participation in drama

This is an excellent way for a boy to take off his mask without fear of ridicule, because the environment is created and safe. It's a place where he can experiment with different behaviours and identities without fear of ostracism from his peers.

Social skills

Give your boy concrete social skills that will enable him to feel relaxed and be himself in the presence of older people. Teach him how to welcome guests into your home; how to introduce them to other guests; how to offer them some refreshment and make them feel relaxed; how to shake someone's hand firmly, but not aggressively, while looking them in the eye; how to establish and carry on a conversation – beginning with showing an interest in the other person.

Encourage him to learn self-defence

This empowers him to know that he can defend himself or others and also teaches him self-control.

Chapter 11

Boys and spirituality, traditions and rites of passage

The modern secular entertainment industry spends billions of dollars a year to profane the sacred: the sacredness of life and the sacredness of our origins.

— Michael Guillen, Harvard lecturer, PhD in maths, physics and astronomy

You are as great as your faith and as small as your ego.

— Shimon Perez, former PM of Israel

It seems to me that, in this generation, we need to make a deliberate effort to reclaim the sacred for our children. It is important that we don't leave our children in a spiritual vacuum and, in the process, rob them of the wonder and connection that comes from our varied spiritual traditions.

Even in a materialistic and secular culture, there are windows of opportunity that allow us to tune in to a child's need to make sense of the world, and to answer the big questions about life that little people as well as intuitive and enquiring teenagers still look to us to help them understand. Who am I? What am I here for? Where am I going?

It may mean going on our own spiritual journey. If we have never taken a good look at the great truths of Christianity and the other religions, or thought deeply about the meaning of life, then the parenting of your sons could be a great time to do this.

Recently, while babysitting, I joined in the reading of a children's version of John Bunyan's *Pilgrim's Progress* with our six-year-old grandson. He briefly told me about Pilgrim's journey so far — that Pilgrim had just reached the Delectable Mountains, where he was watched over by shepherds whose names were Watchful, Experience and Knowledge. I thought about those names and realised why wisdom from past generations still made so much sense. We parents still need to be the 'watchful' shepherds of 'experience' and 'knowledge' for our children. I was fascinated by the way that this ancient classic grabbed our grandson's imagination and satisfied a desire in him for truth.

As we feed our children's minds and encourage learning and the acquisition of knowledge, we must not neglect their hearts. Our children want to know who they are and where they belong, what heaven is like and why God isn't married.

Allowing our boys to become searchers for truth and meaning is part of our coaching role. Without some understanding of the sacred and the wonder of life, everything becomes reduced to 'thing' and 'function', rather than 'meaning' and 'purpose', and we pave the way for the next generation to adopt a philosophy of mere utilitarianism. Are we happy for them to look at life through that lens? A pragmatic balancing of 'usefulness' rather than valuing others for who they are? We should be teaching them that every individual is an amazingly designed person with intrinsic dignity, with their own special mission in the world.

Is there a purpose behind it all? Are our bodies just machines? Or are our bodies beautifully designed for a purpose — to be the container for something so much more precious — our mind and heart? Is sex so much more than a mere biological act? Is it designed by a loving creator, to fulfil our deep needs for love and intimacy? If we don't address some of these deep issues, then our boys' moral code will be rooted in shallow soil.

Deep in our hearts, all of us probably feel that there is more significance to our lives than just eventual fancy fertiliser for the geraniums on our grave. It is easy to push aside these thoughts, but our children force us to address them. Our children should also prod us to consider the eventual outcomes we long to see in our sons, from the investment and love of our parenting. Don't be afraid of the big questions. Read books at the dinner table that will instigate debate and understanding. If you don't know where to find those books, go on a hunt — some of them are mentioned in this book, but there are many other wonderful sources of discussion in life's big questions.

Viktor Frankl, considered one of the great thinkers of the past generation, a survivor of four concentration camps and a practising psychiatrist at the time, crystallised his philosophy of 'life' in the horror of those surroundings. In that environment of desperation, despair and death, he miraculously found 'the indispensable importance of the meaning in life'. This great discovery saved his own life, gave meaning to the suffering of his fellow prisoners and contributed to future generations an invaluable legacy of insight into human nature.

He discovered that, whatever circumstances or cruelty he was subjected to, no one could take away his ultimate freedom of choice; the freedom to choose one's attitude about life and its purpose. In summary, circumstances do not control who we are or who we become. Frankl was able to keep alive a vision of his wife and their love for each other, which became like a beacon for him to rise above his outward agony and pain. He said that many of those who saw 'meaning in life' and envisioned a future, survived. But, in his words, 'Woe to him who saw no more sense to life, no aim, no purpose, and therefore no point in carrying on — he was soon lost.' He added, 'We had to teach the despairing men that it did not really matter what one expected from life, but rather what life expected from us.'

As I have suggested earlier in this book, every boy wants a mission in life — he wants to be brave, to be courageous and to sense that his life counts. So why do we have so many young men who are suicidal or just individualistic hedonists? Could it be that we have not given them a vision of their future, and included them in the world of men who can mentor them into that future? Could it be that they don't feel significant and connected to something bigger than themselves? Could it be that, along with a 'self' to live with and work to live for, we haven't given them a faith to live by, or a cause greater than themselves to live for? Perhaps even a sense of something really worth dying for — so they don't take their own lives over a broken relationship or the humiliation of a bad mistake.

> Every boy wants a mission in life — he wants to be brave, to be courageous and to sense that his life counts. So why do we have so many young men who are suicidal?

I don't mean to denigrate the pain that young men feel when rotten things happen, but we must make them see that there are other options, and that one of those options may be to spend their lives in a meaningful way, in pursuit of a worthy dream or great cause.

The last generation has not been very good at passing on their faith to their children. They often clung to outmoded contexts and ways of doing things. Their children, sensing the lack of relevance in some of these structured idioms, unfortunately discarded important truths and traditions along with the context. However, for parents who want their children to have a faith and to know the truths of their traditions, there are some really innovative ways that modern families can integrate spiritual truths and pass on values.

I recently spent some time co-speaking with Jim Weidmann, an ex-air force pilot, who is passionate about this idea and who has produced a series of 'family night tool-chest' books for parents who want something concrete to build on.

Jim trains parents to be pro-active in this neglected area and he gets very excited about traditions. He feels the modern rejection of old traditions in the home and community has thrown the baby out with the bathwater.

'We have forgotten that most traditions served worthwhile purposes of teaching and preserving good things within a culture,' he says. So, rather than discarding the bathwater, Jim's been heating it up, and adding some bubbles and toys! He sees tradition as being an invaluable tool to pass on to children the heritage they deserve from their parents — a heritage of values and faith. Like any inheritance, heirs are free to do with it as they wish; our children might eventually discard their heritage, modify it or embrace it as a treasure, but it's their right to receive it in the first place — and a parent's duty to pass it on.

I was fascinated listening to some ways he has integrated the old with the new, by resurrecting old traditions, borrowing them from other cultures and inventing new ones.

The secret to children absorbing and embracing your values tends to be the atmosphere. Where ideas are communicated in an environment of affection, order and fun, parents barely need to do any teaching. Intentional, planned family nights are a great way to make this happen — the fun and games hook your kids in and keep them interested, and it's the memorable experience of the object lesson that creates the learning experience.

Over the years I've read many studies where children have been asked what they like best about their families. 'Doing things together' is almost always top of the children's lists.

We were reminded of this truth during a recent visit from our small grandsons. The eldest, a real 'ideas' child, announced they were going to have 'family night' that night as it was Sunday. As his mind ticked on he suggested, 'Granddad, why don't we have family night at your place? You're our family!' Then both boys began to bounce around like little balls saying, 'Yes, let's! Granddad do you know what we do on family nights?'

That evening we had the most fun we've had for a while! After some discussion, the little boys and their dad chose from their 'repertoire' what the family night topic it would be. The story of 'Josh and the Big Wall' won out and, after dinner, the little boys set to work, gathering up all the pillows and cushions they could find and building a huge wall blocking one end of our hallway from the other. Together we sat on the floor and read the story of Joshua and the battle of Jericho. At the right time the little boys blew pretend trumpets, and then single-handedly pushed the wall of pillows over, on to the cheering and wailing semi-smothered adults on the other side.

A little chat about what we'd learned was followed by a fantastic pillow battle between grandfather, father and grandsons, ending with heaps of giggles and hugs. We wouldn't have missed that interchange with our grandchildren for a trip to Disneyland, because it reminded us again that it's the connecting and fun moments that build family culture. And it's through family culture that we communicate the values we want our children to build their lives on.

Deliberately planned times with your boys will create the loving and harmonious environment in your home that lingers in a child's heart for a lifetime. Without it, rather than accepting and absorbing your values and faith, children will more likely react against them.

Between the ages of seven and fifteen, peaking at thirteen, children are most receptive to values and beliefs. They develop their 'moral compass', their sense of right and wrong, at a young age, and it seldom alters as they grow older. Most will not significantly alter their moral outlook and religious beliefs after their teenage years.

Few would disagree that we need good men who possess their own strong moral compass to lead future generations. Unfortunately, unless we consider this important, there a million things in our busy culture that will distract us from this intentional passing on of values.

You can create a heritage for your children

Deliberately or not, the lives we parents live out in front of our children have a powerful influence them, and the families they will have. We are the product of our emotional heritage, and 97 percent of us parent the way we were parented. Sadly, alcoholics raise alcoholics, abusers raise abusers. But it is not an unchangeable doom — because we can change in one generation.

If you wish, you can rethink what you are doing as a parent. You can do things differently from what you knew as a child.

Through many of the things we did with our children, I experienced a family life that, in many ways, helped me re-parent myself. Mary suggested picnics in the back garden, family times around the dinner table and many little traditions around festivals such as Christmas and Easter. I often resisted these at first because they were unfamiliar and a bit of an effort but, looking back, it was those proactive, planned family times that created a wonderful family culture, and many memories that still make us smile.

Traditions move a child through the maturation process

Traditions identify your family. They give boys a sense of who they are and what they belong to.

The father in *Fiddler on the Roof* summed it up, in his own expressive, personal way. 'Traditions . . . aah . . . why traditions? . . . Because they tell me who I am and,' looking up, he adds, 'who He is!'

Traditions that escort boys out of childishness and welcome them into the solemn duties and wonderful privileges of manhood are common to many cultures. Formality and ritual make such traditions meaningful. The whole community coming together for the purpose of acknowledging one person gives that person a great feeling of self worth. Jewish men, for instance, talk of the valuable sense of transition gained from going through the bar mitzvah ceremony at age thirteen.

Some cultures have similar ceremonies for girls, but they are far more common for boys. Perhaps this is because boys need to 'cross over' from the world of women into the world of men.

Coming-of-age rituals for boys share some typical elements; the focus of the whole community is solely on the boy, there is a sense of the special or 'sacred'; both the 'elders' and the boy's father are present, but the father is not in control and does not intercede or speak for his son. There are sometimes elements of risk and fear, such as a lonely vigil at night. There are also often tests and ordeals to prove courage or intelligence. In a tribal context it might mean a hunt, in the bar mitzvah it's chanting or reading from the Torah. Mentors are provided to give ongoing training. The ceremony marks membership of a new group, and afterwards the young man is treated differently. Depending on the culture, he'll also have some outward sign of his new status, such as a feather, tattoo, or long trousers!

Many of these ceremonies and rituals have been lost in our 21st-century society. We may still have 21st-birthday parties, but for many it's just an excuse for a booze-up. A lot of boys never experience a formal transition to manhood, but they retain a glimmer of understanding about the need for this, and unconsciously seek events and 'ceremonies' that mark them as men. It might be proving their manhood by being able to drink a yard-glass of beer, or 'scoring' for the first time. It might be proving their courage in a street race or a fight. All-night rave parties, drug experiences, tattooing and the risks associated with extreme sports all have initiation connotations. The huge difference is that these 'de facto' rites of passage are with same-age peers, and not with men or elders. There might be altered consciousness, but no sense of the sacred. There might be new experiences, but they don't impart any new life-equipping knowledge.

> A lot of boys never experience a formal transition to manhood, but they retain a glimmer of understanding about the need for this.

Growing up involves separation from parents, and the gap year is now an expected part of the experience of growing up in New Zealand and elsewhere. So is going away to another city for work or tertiary study. Again, these look like steps towards the world of maturity but, in reality are frequently steps into protracted immaturity. The 'great leap into adulthood' is often followed by a 'great leap back home' until debt is paid off. Poet and sociologist Robert Bly writes in his book, *Sibling Society*, 'People don't bother to grow up, and we are all fish swimming in a tank of half-adults, with no responsibilities to assume and no long-term commitments to undertake.'

'Thirty is the new twenty-one', goes the saying. Many young people now routinely expect to enjoy a decade of selfish irresponsibility in their twenties before settling into adult life. Much of this protracted childhood is at the expense of parents, who find themselves saddled with 'Kippers' — Kids In Parents' Pockets Eroding Retirement Savings.

The whole process of becoming a man has been carefully thought through by people like Rex McCann, of the Essentially Men Network. He says, 'An appropriate rite of passage helps shift a young man from boy psychology to man psychology . . . It links him to a sense of purpose and feeling of belonging in his wider community.'

McCann has developed a 'Pathways' programme for boys and their fathers that creates a sense of community in a bush camp setting. The time together provides valuable opportunities for men who are positive role models to tell their stories, and for boys to listen and learn. It uses powerful and adventurous processes in time-honoured ways. 'Young men connect with the three core questions they'll be asking themselves over the next seven years: Who am I? Where am I going? Who is going with me?'

In thinking about what sort of men we want our boys to become, McCann has identified a few of the things universally recognised as elements of true manhood. They include:

- Moving from egocentricity to concern for others.
- Facing up to mortality.
- Moving to respect-based behaviour, rather than shame- or fear-based behaviour.
- Developing a social conscience.
- Learning that showing you care is not a vulnerability.
- Being discerning about whom you trust.
- Standing up for what you believe, and speaking for yourself.
- Having integrity.
- Learning to live with failure and disappointment.
- Learning to handle fear (Fear is normal and okay. When it has passed, you'll still be there).
- Going against the Hollywood code as regards sexuality (It's sacred and involves commitment).
- Owning your own mistakes.

Ideally, rites of passage should take place within the context of a wider community. This immediately throws up the question 'What community?' In modern New Zealand, like in the UK, we have a growing population but a decreasing sense of belonging, especially of communities where individuals function in the role of 'respected elder'. As my colleague John Cowan says, 'I just can't imagine getting the people of Torbay (the Auckland suburb where he lives) out into a park for a midnight bonfire and initiation ceremony for my kids.'

A suburb is rarely a community of connected souls with a collective sense of responsibility to each other. Schools are one of the few communities that nearly all of us with children have an association with.

I especially like the concept practised in Melbourne's Xavier College, where they provide two-month courses for their fourteen-year-olds on what it means to be a man. Once the course is done, the boys go on a ski trip with their dads. Then they are welcomed back to the school with a special meal, where the men introduce their sons. We could do more of this kind of thing.

There are also social and workplace communities. Admitting a boy into the company of older men as they relax, play sport or work together is incredibly affirming for him.

Finally, there's the community of your own family, where we can acknowledge our boy's growing maturity. We can increasingly give our son responsibility as he is able to handle it. And we can express our pleasure and pride in his progress. Real men are still needed, and worth celebrating.

HOT TIP ✔

Whatever you decide to do as a family, establish rituals while you still have the window of opportunity. You will give your son an identity, a sense of connectedness and continuity, and a future to look forward to.

Milestones

As well as ongoing traditions like family nights woven into regular family life, and those surrounding religious festivals and holidays like Christmas and Easter, you can establish 'milestone' traditions. Some families have a 'preparation for adolescence' at age eleven when, as well as a one-on-one weekend away with dad, a boy is welcomed into adolescence with a special meal and speeches from important people in his life; or a sixteen-year-old's 'rite of passage' which acknowledges competencies, and to which significant mentors are invited.

Some, like the Jewish bar mitzvah, have a long history and tradition, others are also religion based, such as communion or baptism, and others can be your own family's version. More and more modern families are acknowledging that this form of family approval and attention provides a 'blessing' for their sons. This concept is not specific to any culture, but is a universal life-principle of the parental blessing of children at the time of puberty to release them into adulthood, conveying a sense of identity and destiny.

Unfortunately, we often don't have a sense of urgency. We think we have twenty-one years to get this stuff across, and busyness is our biggest enemy. Take my word for it, every minute you invest in this sort of proactive family activity will pay off in a myriad of ways. The positive attention the children receive through family times and healthy rituals will mean bad behaviour is much less of an issue. There will be memories, which may often be retold at family get-togethers (and at your expense). There is also the family loyalty, not to mention the fun of being part of it all.

However, the most gratifying by-product will be the character of your boys. They will know what you believe and are likely to buy in very readily, discussing freely with you at the dinner table the conundrums they face when they are trying to put into practice those values in the real world.

ACTION LAB ⟳

TIPS FOR RITES OF PASSAGE

Window of opportunity

On his fourteenth birthday, have a dinner where you acknowledge he is becoming a young man. Share with your son three things you admire about him, three achievements, and three gifts and talents that he's been blessed with. He then gives a speech and talks about what he considers his three strengths, three things he's been thankful for and his future dreams.

Male blessing

When he is sixteen, plan together with your son a significant evening to mark his birthday.

Invite, with his consultation, up to five mentors who have played a role in your son's life. (They may be his granddads, a sports coach, a youth leader, a family friend, for example.)

Ask each mentor to bring a small gift which represents a piece of 'life wisdom', to hand on to your son. (For example, granddad may bring a coffee mug and say something like 'Son, I have learned that in life people will give you plenty of valuable free advice; you just have to ask. I have learnt that it is usually over a cup of coffee!')

After dinner, each of these friends and mentors will explain their gift and then your son will give a speech, thanking each one for the input they have had in his life.

This is the type of male blessing that marks a true 'rite of passage' for your boy.

IN SUMMARY 👁

WHAT ALL BOYS NEED

All boys need:

- A sense of purpose and meaning.
- A passage through to adulthood.
- A way of moving from boy psychology to man psychology.
- Strong connections to the family and community.
- A spiritual compass.
- Answers to the big questions in life.
- A great cause to commit their life to.
- A family heritage.
- Rites of passage that identify and affirm their growing maturity.

Chapter 12

Twelve things I want my boys to know

During the sixties and seventies, a generation of parents who'd rebelled against societal norms and the standards of their parents began experimenting with different ways to bring up their kids. A relatively values-free approach to child rearing became the norm for many. However, as children who have grown up without boundaries are picking up the pieces of their sometimes chaotic lives, there appears to have been a bit of a swing back. Educators and parents recognise the value of mentoring, boundaries and a sense of the future as passed on by loving and firm parents. I like to call this 'intentional parenting'.

Did your parents have sayings and mottos that they repeated until they became family lore? Sayings such as 'Work is its own reward' or 'The output is the input less resistance losses' or 'Think before you speak'? These are concepts each generation can build on. Teenagers may discard your so-called 'wisdom' if they sense hypocrisy or excessive control but, more likely than not, your life lessons will give them a platform to launch themselves from, without their having to learn every lesson themselves through painful consequences.

Here are twelve truths that, as an 'intentional dad', I wanted my kids to learn. You may also consider them worth handing on. I originally sourced these from an article by Jerry Jenkins and have used them many times over the years.

1. Set only essential goals

Many teenagers have so many goals and dreams that they don't focus on any of them, and their youthful energy becomes dissipated. Encourage teenagers to focus on the *essential* goals, such as getting into a sports team of their choice or passing a music exam.

2. Know what love is

Our modern world has confused love with sex, and we need to make sure our children understand the difference. Love is about friendship, faithfulness and sacrifice. It's essentially about actions not feelings. The media preaches that if you have sex you will find intimacy. In fact, only when you cultivate intimacy in a committed relationship will sex be truly meaningful.

3. Never quit

Too many people get off the train in the middle of the tunnel. We need to teach our children that if we want to achieve anything we must expect adversity. Our support and high expectations can help kids stick with any commitment if it gets tough.

4. Some people have the right to be wrong

Usually the boss! Testing and challenging norms and standards is part of being a teenager — but so is living in the real world. Respecting other people and authority where it's appropriate is how society works. Teenagers may want to give advice to those who supervise them, but there are respectful and appropriate ways to communicate.

5. Life isn't fair

The sooner our boys understand this truth, the easier life will be for them. There is injustice and unfairness in everyday life. The skill is learning to live with what cannot be changed right away and working toward what can possibly be changed in the future.

6. Take responsibility for your own actions

It's called 'living with the consequences', and people who do this will succeed in life. It's also a powerful tool in building self-esteem. Support your children as they learn the difficult but important lessons that come with 'messing up'. Your empathy, without anger, will help them to connect the consequence with the action, and to help them make a better choice next time. Is it kind? Is it true? Is it necessary?

7. Watch your tongue

Words cannot be swallowed. Although the tongue is a small part of our body, it's like a match that can light a forest fire. Better to think twice before you speak.

8. Work before you play; but play

To work first and then play is the way successful people operate. It's especially important, when you get married, to know that not only commitment and love, but also fun, keep a relationship together. Celebrate life, and model play to your boys. A favourite family game as a reward for when all the chores are done will keep you connected even during the teenage years.

9. Women work harder than men

What can I say? Simply that we men can gain a lot of appreciation by acknowledging this. If we encourage the women in our lives to take breaks and offer to help out so that they can, our relationships with them will be enriched.

10. Play to your strengths

Develop those things that you are naturally good at and become competent and knowledgeable. If you win the creative writing contest at school but never make the first eleven, then your best strengths may not be in sport but in the literary field. Enjoy the esteem that comes from the acknowledgement of your strengths, and don't compare yourself with those who have different talents.

11. Some things are black and white

Relativism, or believing what's right in your own eyes, is a nice thought, but a myth. There are absolute truths, such as the law of gravity, and there are some beliefs that have more credibility and better outcomes than others.

12. Cultivate a best friend

Friendship doesn't just happen. It needs to be cultivated. If you want great friends, you first need to be a great friend. Take the initiative in friendships, and give them a high priority.

Intentional parents have dreams for their kids. When my children were young I wanted them to grow up to be givers rather than takers, to influence society for good and to be respected by their fellow human beings.

I think the poem on the opposite page sums it all up. Often quoted as being by Mother Teresa, it was actually written by Kent M. Keith, a student leader in the 1970s. It gives young people some worthy goals.

The Anyway Poem

People are often unreasonable, illogical, and self-centred.
Forgive them anyway.
If you are kind, people may accuse you of selfish, ulterior motives.
Be kind anyway.
If you are successful, you may win some false friends and some true
enemies.
Succeed anyway.
If you are honest and frank, people may cheat you.
Be honest and frank anyway.
Transparency may make you vulnerable.
Be transparent anyway.
If you find serenity and happiness, others may be jealous.
Be happy anyway.
What you spend years building may be destroyed overnight.
Build anyway.
The good you do today may be forgotten tomorrow.
Do good anyway.
People who really want help may attack you if you help them.
Help them anyway.
Give the world the best you have and it may never be enough.
Give the world your best anyway.
You see, in the final analysis, it is between you and God.
It is never between you and them anyway.

More good reading

Biddulph, Steve, *Raising Boys*, London, Thorsons, 2003.

Biddulph, Steve, *Manhood*, London, Vermilion, 2004.

Bly, Robert, *Sibling Society*, London, Penguin Books Ltd, 1997.

Bowlby, John, *Attachment and Loss*, London, Pimlico, 1998.

Carson, Ben, *Gifted Hands*, Grand Rapids, Zondervan Books, 1990.

Cline, Foster and Fay, Jim, *Parenting with Love and Logic*, Colorado Springs, Piñon Press, 2006.

Coloroso, Barbara, *Kids Are Worth It*, London, HarperCollins Publishers, 2002.

Cooper, Scott, *Sticks and Stones: seven ways your child can deal with teasing, conflict and other hard times*, New York, Times Books, 2000.

Dobson, James, *Bringing Up Boys*, Wheaton, Tyndale House Publishers, 2001.

Eldredge, John, *Wild At Heart*, Nashville, Nelson Books, 2006.

Frankl, Viktor, *Man's Search for Meaning*, London, Rider & Co, 2004.

Grant, Ian and Cowan, John, *Parenting Teenagers: The Whitewater Rafting Years*, Rozelle; Auckland, Pa's Publishing, 1999.

Green, Christopher, *Beyond Toddlerdom*, London, Vermilion, 2007.

Gurian, Michael, *The Good Son*, New York, Jeremy P. Tarcher, 1999.

Gurian, Michael, *The Wonder of Boys*, New York, Putnam, 1996.

Hunter, Brenda, *The Power of Mother Love*, Colorado Springs, Waterbook Press, 1998.

Kindlon, D. and Thompson, M., *Raising Cain: protecting the emotional life of boys*, London, Ballantine Books, 2000.

Kuzma, Kay, *Building Your Child's Character from the Inside Out*, Chariot Family Publishing, 1988.

Lashlie, Celia, *He'll Be OK: growing gorgeous boys into good men*, Auckland, HarperCollins, 2005.

Lewis, C.S., *The Four Loves*, London, Fount, 2002.

Marsden, John, *Secret Men's Business: manhood, the big gig*, Sydney, Pan Macmillan, 1998.

Mayle, Peter, *'What's Happening To Me?'*, London, Citadel Press, 2001.

McGinnis, Alan Loy, *The Friendship Factor: how to get closer to the people you care for*, Minneapolis, Augsberg Publishing House, 1979.

Morton, Tom, *Altered Mates: the man question*, St Leonards, Allen and Unwin, 1997.

Murray, Jenni, *That's My Boy!*, London, Vermilion, 2003

O'Reilly, Bill, *The O'Reilly Factor for Kids: a survival guide for America's families*, New York, HarperEntertainment, 2004.

Pollack, William, *Real Boys: rescuing our sons from the myths of boyhood*, New York, Henry Holt & Company, 1999.

Popenoe, David, *Life Without Father*, London, Simon & Schuster, 1997.

Schlessinger, Laura, *How Could You Do That?*, New York, HarperCollins, 1996.

Seligman, Martin, *The Optimistic Child: proven programme to safeguard children from depression and build lifelong resilience*, Boston, Houghton Mifflin, 1995.

Stuart, Timothy and Stuart, Mona, *Raising Children at Promise*, San Francisco, Jossey-Bass, 2005.

Wilson, James, *The Moral Sense*, London, Pocket Books, 1998.

CD

Cowan, John and Hale, Jenny, *The Big Weekend*, Parents Inc.

Website

www.attitude.org.nz

Index